The
TurboCharged
Mind

"With its straightforward advice, easy-to-follow food rules, and boundless encouragement, TurboCharged stands out from the rest of the diet and exercise guidebooks by digging deep into topics like body mass, metabolism, and eating habits. … With its numerous tips, real-life examples, well-articulated advice, and 'you can do it' encouragement, TurboCharged can help anyone get on track with diet and exercise."

- Elizabeth Millard
ForeWord Reviews

★★★★★"There are very few body improvement books that can be recommended more highly than TURBOCHARGED. Even reading the book is addictive and to say much more about the book would be a disservice to those out there who are frustrated with fatty deposits in their bodies. Buy your own copy, keep our own copy for reference, and encourage your acquaintances with healthy outlooks who are struggling with expensive diets and special meals and memberships in programs to buy it too. This book works!"

- Grady Harp
Vine Voice
Top 10 Amazon Reviewer

"A Top 10 Metabolism and Diet Book. One of my all time favorites."

- Conner V. James
Listmania!

"Beyond a consummate presentation, the Griesels excite and motivate the reader to toss the treats and embrace the plan. Those ready for an extreme makeover will hit the TurboCharged trail and stay there. An inspiring, upbeat guide to beating fat for good."

- Kirkus Reviews

"The TurboCharged program seems to be one that you can adopt for a lifetime."

- Diets in Review.com

"Fantastic! There is a weight loss program I can follow and not have to use supplements, have to exercise 'til I feel like dying, or radically change the way I eat. I think this is amazing, and if a person really stuck with it, it works! The book is easy to follow and understand."

- Hanging Off the Wire

"We live in a society where we are quite literally eating ourselves to death. Everyone says they want to "lose weight," but what we really need is to lose fat. TurboCharged puts the emphasis on body-fat percentage—a true indicator of your state of health and risk for certain food-related diseases, such as heart disease and stroke. The authors' concept of the land of Leandom and the highway traveling there is a fantastic way to present what every one of us ultimately wants: to be lean and healthy."

- Fred Pescatore, MD, MPH, CCN
Best-selling Author of The Hamptons Diet
(Excerpt from his TurboCharged Foreword)

"Finally you can toss the exercise DVDs, failed diet programs, useless equipment and take control of your body! TurboCharged is what we've all been waiting for: a simple approach to better living and a powerful new lifestyle."

- Harvey Schiller, Ph.D,
Brig. Gen., USAF, Ret.
Former CEO, United States
Olympic Committee

The
TurboCharged
Mind

Eliminate Bad Habits with Hypnosis

DIAN GRIESEL, Ph.D with TOM GRIESEL

THE BUSINESS SCHOOL OF HAPPINESS

CONNECTICUT

TurboCharged is a trademark of The Business School of Happiness, Inc.

For information contact:
Business School of Happiness, Inc.
Attn: Permissions Dept.
P.O. Box 302
Washington Depot, CT 06794
860.619.0177

Published by The Business School of Happiness Inc.
Cover and Interior Design by Carla Rood
Cover Graphic from 123rf.com
Editing by Sebastian Thaler
Made in The United States of America

Turbocharged books and meditations may be purchased and downloaded directly from www.turbocharged.us.com. For further information, call 860.619.0177 or visit our websites at www.businessschoolofhappiness.com or www.turbocharged.us.com.

Substantial discounts on bulk quantities are available to corporations, professional associations and other organizations. For details and discount information, contact our special sales department.

PLEASE NOTE: The creators and publishers of this book are not and will not be responsible, in any way whatsoever, for the improper use made by anyone of the information contained in this book. All use of the aforementioned information must be made in accordance with what is permissible by law, and any damage liable to be caused as a result thereof will be the exclusive responsibility of the user. In addition, he or she must adhere strictly to the safety rules contained within the book, both in training and in actual implementation of the information presented herein. TurboCharged and The TurboCharged Mind are companion books. They constitute a healthful program for rapid body-fat loss and greater wellbeing. Neither book makes any medical claims. It is the sole responsibility of every person planning to apply the techniques described in these books to consult a licensed physician in order to obtain complete medical information on his or her personal ability and limitations. The instructions and advice printed in these books are not in any way intended as a substitute for medical, mental or emotional counseling with a licensed physician or healthcare provider. Before beginning any part of the TurboCharged program, we suggest that when you consult your physician you request a complete physical along with full blood-panel testing. These numbers will serve as an excellent baseline to measure your progress as you follow this program.

ISBN # 978-1-936705-05-4
Library of Congress applied for and pending.

Dedication

To all of those we know and love who help to keep our minds, hearts and bodies TurboCharged in countless ways on a daily basis.

Contents

Preface

Dian and I both have an insatiable desire to understand how our human "vehicle" works. Always learning, we never cease to be amazed by the body's marvelous ability to function and adapt to a perpetually changing environment. We search continuously for understanding and to grasp the keys that will help turn our bodies "on" to operate at optimal levels, while conversely to comprehend those factors that contribute to the "crashes" or collapse of basic, innate functions. Our search and research is driven by our belief that uncovering universal bodily requirements is critical for living life in high gear with unstoppable optimal health.

Endless reading and research with respect to health, wellbeing and longevity has been both eye and mind opening on many levels. It has also firmly convinced us that in order to make any lasting change for betterment, we must start with our self-image. Self-image is your personal guidance system and it is housed deep in your unconscious mind.

When I was younger, I smoked cigarettes. I knew quitting was a logical and reasonable decision because a high incidence of cancer ran in my family, with cigarette smoking being the common thread. Yet, in spite of this very conscious knowledge, along with desire and what I thought was strong "will-power", I did quit often, for short periods of time, only to start smoking again. This pattern continued for quite longer than one might reason-ably expect. Apparently, I would soon forget the "reasons" I wanted to quit and would ultimately resume the habit. When I began to read about the workings of the subconscious mind, I started to understand that I had a firmly entrenched, stored self-image of a smoker. I had internalized various messages that were conflicting, yet nonetheless created a wholly unconscious and detrimental imprint in my mind. By learning to incorporate a simple method to "re-program" my self-image from a smoker to a non-smoker, change came quickly and I never relapsed into smoking and more remarkably, never missed a cigarette. Over the years, I have taught the technique to many people and they all kicked the habit with the same ease and permanency. I have often used the simple method to change other habits as well for the better and have always been amazed with the results.

Dian became an advanced level clinical hypnotherapist as a complimentary extension of her nutritional counseling practice. Using the same methods we reveal in this book and in our TurboCharged Mind Hypnosis download series, Dian has witnessed amazing results and transformations with countless individuals.

In *TurboCharged: Accelerate Your Fat Burning Metabolism, Get Lean Fast and Leave Diet and Exercise Rules in the Dust* we dedicated one of the 8 steps entirely to "Seeing the Prize" which addresses the importance of relaxation, meditation and visualization. Because this information is so critical to success, we actually thought about making it step #1. Due to limited space and scope, we barely scratched the surface and resolved to make more detailed and critical information along with effective techniques available to our readers. *The TurboCharged Mind* is the fruit of our efforts.

Dian is the expert when it comes to hypnosis and she will be your guide in explaining its intricacies and applications. Early on we knew we wanted to create a series of self-hypnosis downloads for not only fat-loss but many other life changes people were interested in making. This book shares our collective knowledge and experience. Like space travel, *The TurboCharged Mind* opens the doorway to "a whole new unexplored frontier" just waiting to be used fruitfully for your ultimate benefit.

At the end of each chapter we have included a summary called

TurboCharged Mind Seeds… We use the word seeds because these are key points and thoughts that we want you to plant in both your conscious and subconscious minds. These simple review points will help to install and reinforce positive new ideas in your brain that will then result in positive changes in your body, mind and life.

When I first listened to the *TurboCharged™ Beginner Meditation* download recording that Dian created, I knew we were on the right track and the new series would become a valuable resource for change in any area of your life. To help you start this journey, at www.turbocharged.us.com, in the Store, we are giving away this download free of charge so you can begin to experience the awesome power of self-hypnosis right away.

All change begins in our minds with the thoughts or "seeds" we choose to plant there. Get ready to explore and experience an exciting new dimension of possibilities in your life.

-*Tom Griesel*

Introduction

I experienced hypnosis for my first time twenty years ago. I asked the hypnotist to focus my guided meditation session on increasing my sense of powerful positive energy regardless of the situation or circumstance. My sense of relaxation during the session was immensely peaceful and that alone was wonderful. But more remarkable, was that I felt deeply and truly transformed on some unidentifiable level. I literally felt positively powerful! Although I have never been able to exactly pinpoint the how's or 'why's of the experience or describe it to another justifiably, that marked sense of transformation has been with me ever since. It also sent me on a twenty-year ongoing mission to learn everything possible about hypnosis and how it can benefit or "trance"-form my daily experience of life and that of others as well.

Today, besides having a Ph.D. in nutritional science, I am certified as an advanced clinical hypnotherapist. I have attended over 100 continuing education workshops over the years and still enjoy learning from the books written by some of the greatest explorers of the subconscious mind. Much of their thinking has penetrated both my conscious and unconscious thoughts and is relayed throughout the pages of this book along with my own observations. So please, if you enjoy this book, do take the time to read the fabulous works of others that can be found in the bibliography.

Hypnosis is the most exciting, quickest, easiest and most effective way to create positive change in your life. It allows us to "open up" the elusive subconscious mind that drives our behaviors. Much like a GPS system in a car whereby you input your desired destination and ultimately arrive on schedule, hypnosis, once experienced and reinforced, is completely automatic.

You identify your goal – taking off 20+ pounds of excess body fat…sleeping restfully through the night…breaking the smoking addiction…regaining your self-confidence…decreasing stress and increasing relaxation…or whatever you wish – then you listen to a guided meditation download or work with a professional hypnotist, and seemingly like magic the suggestion is suddenly burned deeply into both your subconscious and conscious minds.

The rest is completely automatic! Seriously, you read that right—automatic. Your subconscious must and will strive toward its assigned mission until the goal is reached. You need not even think about it, once you have started practicing self-hypnosis. Instead, you simply go about your daily life as usual as your subconscious works diligently night and day toward the goal(s) you have set.

If you are intrigued, please keep reading. I'll begin by identifying much of the mystery that surrounds hypnosis, dispel the myths and misinformation and then explain clearly and concisely how this elementary phenomenon can literally change your life almost effortlessly for the better.

I realize this may sound too good to be true. But if you are at all intrigued, don't quit now. This book is a short, quick and easy read. Hopefully you'll find it interesting, too. It comes with a promise: If you read it from start to finish you will see yourself in an entirely new, more kind and compassionate way. With no mumbo-jumbo, but instead the straight talk you already know Tom and I espouse, you will be well on your way to achieving with greater ease whatever it is that would bring you more health, happiness, wellbeing and other countless miscellaneous benefits. You will be grateful for the day this book found its way into your hands.

-*Dian Griesel, Ph.D.*

1

"Free Your Mind and the Rest Will Follow"

—En Vogue, 1992

Quite often it is very difficult, if not impossible, to think clearly. Clearly without prejudice, that is, or without preconceived notions. Many decisions that we make are not "freewill" decisions. Most of us have brains that are encumbered with heavy chains that bind us to all the people who have had profound effects on our lives. Parents, teachers, friends, bosses, associates—along with anyone we've been exposed to, whether we respected and liked them or not—have left their mark in our conscious and unconscious minds. Think about this: Have you ever said something and almost immediately realized that your comment sounded more like one of your parents' utterances than your own? Have you ever said something to a child that you swore you would never say because your parents had—such as, "Eat that dinner! There are starving people in..." Or have you ever made a statement in a matter-of-fact way, and suddenly felt a little inkling in the back of your mind that maybe, what you have always stated or believed to be a fact—because of what you have been told—just might not be so? Has anyone ever questioned some aspect of your behavior, while you argued and rationalized that you have "always done it this way?" If you can relate to any of this, or have had experiences anything like these examples— you are not alone. All of us, invariably, have incorporated into our daily routine, comments and opinions that are not necessarily reflections of how we really feel, but rather tokens and relics of our upbringing and development.

As we develop and grow up, believing we are becoming "free-thinking," independent individuals, it becomes apparent that in many ways, both conscious and unconscious, we are not so free-thinking after all. Please don't construe this as an insult. It's basically a fact of life. We all suffer the effects of the socialization process.

As children, we are all told—and "conditioned" to the idea— that we have to get along with others. Often, those who guided us were well-intentioned people who were busy, lacking time, tired and stressed—much like many of us today. As a result, we learned that when we acted from "who we are," we got into trouble. We were told to "listen, I know, I have experience," and to ignore our own perceptions and realities. Not complying with the directions we were being given often meant that we got in trouble. Accordingly, we either began to believe that something was wrong with us, or we simply decided that we didn't want to get in trouble again. So to avoid the wrath of others, we began to alter who we are, what we believe, what we say, and what we do to be more in line with the beliefs of others. We did this because on some level, we believed this would make life easier. Somehow, the fact that we are all "human beings"…got lost along our way to adulthood. None of this is our own fault or anyone else's. It's just the process of human existence. We all have egos. We all think we know something and can make someone's life better. So, like it or not, all that others have shared with us—whether with good or bad intentions—results in the indisputable fact that we are really not such original thinkers at all. We are each subconsciously ingrained with so many opinions from those we respect and love that they consciously or unconsciously become our own opinions—for better or for worse, for our ultimate pain or pleasure, for satisfying or dissatisfying experiences, and for a healthy or unhealthy life. Even as I pass the half-century mark, I hate to accept that I might not be the original thinker I want to believe I am. I'd venture you aren't too thrilled by that possibility, either.

So where does this leave us? Are we doomed to simply be the watered-down product of all of our "influencers," and then, if we are lucky, manage to add a few opinions and perspectives of our own? (To inflict upon others, of course...)

In our opinion, it would take a lifetime (and probably gazillions of dollars for therapy sessions!) to sort out and decipher your original thoughts from those you absorbed from others—if it were really possible at all. That's a long time to be able to assess knowledge and come to a clear, unprejudiced decision on its value. But is this necessary?

Yes and no. Let's put it this way: Yes, it is helpful and rewarding to do some work to free your mind from the shackles that encumber it. And the work is well worth it. Few things in life are more satisfying and comforting than knowing that your decisions and actions truly reflect who you are and how you feel. Not expecting perfection, but rather a kinder version of self-acceptance, through knowing you utilized specific thought processes to draw your conclusions or chart your course.

But at the same time, no, it does not have to be super hard and painful to work through a lot of old baggage! Clearing your mind, zeroing in on what is important to you, is actually easier than you might imagine. Really. Now isn't finding out exactly how to do this worth the price of admission?

To re-educate and to discover your "self" begins with thoughtfully considering all evidence as it is presented in the **present** (important word—that's why it's bolded) while learning to delve into the evidence with valid questions. To teach yourself to consider and carefully weigh the merits of ideas, situations or circumstances in the **present** (told you it was important…that's why it's bolded again)—rather than to accept or reject them—until you can determine the validity for yourself. Finally, it involves maintaining a healthy sense of humor along with a lot of self-forgiveness because it is guaranteed that in the present, you'll need to simply laugh sometimes and you may really learn what the word "sorry" means.

As you read the following pages, the goal is to open your mind to the power of your mind. Set aside your preconceived notions that might inhibit you from learning something new and powerful. The most sacred aspect of being human is our ability to think and reason. Assess the assorted data and allow your magnificent brain to make some truly free-willed determinations. In the pages that follow, you will learn how to free your mind, to open it to new possibilities that already exist. And the best part of all? You really won't need to do anything. Keep reading. Free your mind and the rest will follow.

Chapter 1: TurboCharged Mind Seeds...

◈ Most of your daily functions are accomplished on a sub-conscious level.

◈ Subconscious thoughts are capable of affecting you physically and psychologically.

◈ You are what you believe subconsciously. What your subconscious believes feeds back to your conscious life and determines your behavior patterns.

◈ What you believe subconsciously can determine whether you will be successful or unsuccessful, happy or unhappy, healthy or sick and possibly alive or dead.

◈ Most of us need to be dehypnotized.

2

What Is Hypnosis?

Believe it or not, everyone reading this book has experienced hypnosis. If you're thinking that sounds bold—let me go further. Each of you experiences a hypnotic state at least once a day, and I'd even bet that most of you experience hypnotic states several times a day—each and every day of your lives.

Are you curious about these claims? I hope so. Let me explain. Basically, it's like this: Your brain operates on four different, measurable frequency cycles. Each corresponds to certain kinds of activity. The first cycle, beta, is your conscious mind. This is where we do our reasoning and conduct most of our affairs. We are awake in the beta cycle stage. The next is alpha, which is considered to be our subconscious range. It is during this cycle that you are able to daydream or meditate. Alpha is also the cycle during which nearly all hypnosis takes place. The third cycle is theta. Theta is part of the subconscious range, and hypnosis may occur here—although few people ever get down into theta for very long. Any and all of our emotional experiences are stored in theta. The fourth stage is delta, which is total unconsciousness. Beyond that, not much is known. For our purposes, we are mainly concerned with beta and alpha. Every time you go to sleep, your brain automatically cycles down. It goes from beta range into alpha and once in a while cycles through theta and delta. However, most of your sleep is in alpha.

Let me give you a visual. Can you recall ever experiencing the pleasant sensation that can occur as you lie in bed, just sort of drifting, not really awake yet not really asleep? More likely than not, if you were asked a question while in this state of relaxation, it would take a little longer than usual to answer. Why? Because you would probably be trying to figure out if the voice was part of a dream or not. Have you ever awoken to the sound of your alarm clock, yet in your groggy state imagined that the alarm was a telephone in your dream or a chime signaling the end of class?

What is happening at these times is that your brain is drifting in the alpha range. It is conscious, yet not really. Hypnosis is a simple technique involving strategies to create deep states of relaxation, slowing down the brain cycle from beta to alpha, yet stopping short of sleep. In alpha, the subconscious mind is open to positive suggestions. Hypnosis is a mental state that can involve imaginative role-enactment that takes advantage of this natural phenomenon. This is because in the alpha state, the boundaries of what you may have always believed to be real can be questioned, and positive messages can be sent to redirect your actions to become more helpful to you, more healthful and ultimately more beneficial to your overall wellbeing.

Now I said most of us experience hypnotic states several times a day—so let me explain further. Have you ever gotten into your car to go for a drive and arrived at your destination safely, yet wondered how you got there? Or have you ever driven your car right past your expressway exit, and wondered where the heck you thought you were going? Have you ever walked down the street, oblivious to the activity around you, and felt startled when you heard your name called or when you arrived at your destination unharmed? Have you ever sat mesmerized in front of a television set as someone called your name a couple of times trying to get your attention? These daydreams or hypnotic states are common, and we all experience them almost daily. What makes this possible?

All that you have ever learned is stored in your subconscious. Because you know how to walk and drive, you can saunter down the street, or get in your car and maneuver in and out of traffic. Because these skills are warehoused in your subconscious mind, your conscious mind is free to drift off—and as it does so, your subconscious becomes more active. Consequently, you may become so engrossed in your thoughts that you drive or walk in one direction when you really meant to go in the other. Yet when your attention is required for tollbooths or stoplights, your conscious mind becomes active again.

Driving and walking are only two of many automatic activities. Each time you do anything automatic, your conscious mind is diverted to your subconscious, and it's a good possibility you will go into a hypnotic state. Certain activities—those that seem most basic—allow your mind to drift. Herein lies the key to hypnosis.

Hypnosis is a lot like daydreaming. Anytime you are daydreaming, you are in a state of altered consciousness. Your brain has shifted into the alpha frequency range and consequently enables you to engage in your fantasies. All the while, you are conscious, aware and safe, yet you remain oblivious to external distractions. You are able to fulfill any activity that has become basic to your subconscious mind—driving, walking, watching TV, "spacing out," listening to music and so on. Daydreaming is a perfectly normal, safe and healthy phenomenon. All of us daydream, in some form or another, from time to time.

Daydreaming or fantasizing can be a very positive thing. As

the writer Edgar Allan Poe once said, "Those who dream by day are cognizant of many things that escape those who dream only at night." Some people allow themselves to daydream, unconsciously or in a direct way, so intensely and with such a specific, goal-oriented focus that they are better able to realize their goals. Their elaborate visualization in a relaxed state actually causes the goal to be achieved. This usually happens spontaneously, and often without deliberate intent. Some might call this synchronicity, which Wikipedia defines as the experience that occurs when two or more events that are apparently causally unrelated or unlikely to occur together by chance, are observed to occur together in a meaningful manner.

Hypnosis is a powerful technique for implementing positive changes quickly, and it can be learned and experienced by anyone. To me, it's magical because it enables your brain to slow down and enter the alpha range—which is where dreams occur. Hypnosis allows you to go into this realm of relaxed, altered consciousness—the daydreaming state—and to make your self-directed dreams become realities. Now I'm not saying that you will become a rock star, NHL hockey player, or fulfill any other "dream," because I have no idea what your talents are, or how hard you try or how lucky you are. But I will say that realistic goals—including some that might now be evading your consciousness—are certainly possible. I'll explain.

Like daydreaming, hypnosis is a perfectly normal, safe and healthy phenomenon. Hypnosis mimics that same, highly relaxed state. While under hypnosis, like daydreaming, you are conscious and aware, yet you are able to remain oblivious to external distractions. The only real difference between hypnosis and fantasizing or daydreaming is that in a state of hypnosis, your mind is directed to specific beneficial goals you wish to achieve, and not to fantasies as is the case with daydreaming. By utilizing specific posthypnotic suggestions—either through self-hypnosis with an audio download or by a hypnotherapist—deliberate and direct attention is given to your specific goals so that they will be achieved. Some beneficial goals might be: to quit smoking; lose excess body fat; improve your self-image; relieve stress; overcome phobias and fears; improve memory; enhance your athletic ability; feel more comfortable in crowds; or sleep more restfully. This list is far from complete. There are so many beneficial uses for hypnosis that the list is seemingly endless. I've hypnotized myself and other people for over 20 years. The results never cease to amaze me.

Hypnosis enables you to pump powerful suggestions directly into your subconscious. You see, humans basically have two minds. Picture a wall with a door. On one side of the wall, you have your conscious mind. The conscious mind does the thinking and the "willing." On the other side of the wall you have the unconscious mind. The unconscious sector is responsible for regulating all the major activities necessary for living. It transforms food and oxygen into tissues and energy. It regulates all basic routine functions, such as coordinating the activities of the heart, stomach, liver, kidneys, lungs, and other organs. It is the superintendent of maintenance and repairs broken bones, torn flesh and so on. While the unconscious mind carries out all these activities and functions that we take for granted, it also controls almost all the functions of physical and emotional life. The unconscious mind works with robot efficiency, and we are unaware of all of its vast and complex activity. This arrangement leaves the conscious mind free to attend to all the activities of the outside world.

Now, remember there is a "door in the wall" that separates the two sections of the brain. The conscious mind can be best understood as your will and intellect—kind of like the boss of the body. The subconscious represents the workers. They just keep going about their assigned duties 24 hours a day. The subconscious mind's "workers" will carry out any orders they are given—in addition to maintaining the routine functions of emotional and physical life. Now, back to that door. At the door, imagine a guard, present at all times, whose job is to prevent the workers in the subconscious from getting orders—because they will do whatever they are told, irrespective of what it is or who tells them! The guard is there to censor orders to make sure things don't go haywire. If the guard were not there, anytime you saw an advertisement or commercial telling you to hop on a plane and "come to Jamaica," you would do so—flying away with no understanding of why you decided to take such an impromptu vacation. Every advertisement would be irresistible. You would become an advertiser's dream—rushing out to buy each and every product that you were told could "do the job better."

So do you get the picture? This guard has a pretty important job. Now, where hypnosis comes in is this: If we could somehow lull the guard into an agreeable state and quietly pass messages along to those helpful workers, we could correct any deviations that might be preventing us from living healthy, happy lives. The workers are receptive because they too are always striving to correct any problem that seems to create an imbalance. The first step in lulling the guard into a quiescent state is inducing a state of physical relaxation. When relaxed, your subconscious is able to accept directions and act on them. In part, it does this by informing the conscious mind that there is new information to be acted upon. The conscious mind loves to act on what it already has, so it starts to act on this new information.

The human brain and body are magnificent in structure. So many aspects of its meticulous operation leave us in wonderment. At present, it is not thoroughly understood why hypnosis works and how the subconscious mind brings about the results. However, we do know that it does work, and that it works amazingly well.

Chapter 2: *TurboCharged Mind Seeds...*

◈ Hypnosis is not sleep.

◈ Hypnosis is a normal and natural state.

◈ All phenomena related to hypnosis can be produced in the so-called "waking state."

◈ Most of your daily functions are accomplished on a subconscious level.

◈ All hypnosis is self-hypnosis.

◈ Self-hypnosis is the most effective way to positively change your life...quickly.

◈ When the subconscious becomes convinced of a fact, whether it is true or false, it becomes a reality in your life.

◈ The basic tools of hypnosis are suggestion and imagination.

3

Debunking the Myths

There are many serious misunderstandings about hypnosis. Many of these misunderstandings have been promoted by Dracula and other vampire movies that depict people being transformed into zombie-like creatures by the Count when he says, "Look into my eyes!" While this may make for a classic, exciting movie, it is 100% fiction. Let's set the record straight on a few myths.

1. *A hypnotist has mysterious powers.*
    FALSE. (But I wish!) A hypnotist is an ordinary human being who has been trained and has mastered the skill of utilizing suggestion to bring about desired results.

2. *A person can be hypnotized and can be directed to do things against their will.*
    ABSOLUTELY FALSE! A false rumor perpetuated by Hollywood and stage hypnotists. First of all, no person can be hypnotized against his or her will. It is your choice to enter the trance state and you can always choose to leave it. Anyone who wants to benefit from hypnosis must be

100% cooperative in order for it to work. Secondly, no one in hypnosis can be told to do anything that they would not freely do if not in hypnosis. While hypnotized, you can choose to accept or reject any suggestions given. If anything upsetting is suggested, the hypnotized individual would immediately wake up—by their own choice.

3. *Only weak-minded people can be hypnotized.*
    FALSE again. In fact, the opposite is true. The more intelligent or creative a person is, the easier it is for them to experience hypnosis. Nearly everyone who wants to be hypnotized can be hypnotized. Children, because they have not yet been stifled by too many "do's and don'ts," are usually very receptive to suggestions under hypnosis. They love to use their imagination. I've used hypnosis with my children almost since birth, and now they still will ask for "extra relaxation talk" usually before bedtime. The more active one's imagination, the better the chances of a successful session. Only about 1% of the population cannot be hypnotized; some of this is due to mental deficiency and some is for reasons we don't yet know or understand.

4. *A hypnotized person is in a trance or is unconscious.*
    NOT TRUE at all. Under hypnosis, the individual is aware and quietly awake at all times; in fact, extremely so. The individual has merely focused his/her attention to where the hypnotist directs it, and is oblivious to anything else. In a hypnotized state you can talk, think, hear, act, etc.

5. *A person can get stuck in hypnosis.*
    FALSE. Even if the hypnotist dropped dead after assisting someone into a deep trance or state of hypnosis, the individual would come out of it quite easily. The hypnotized

individual would do one of two things: just open his/ her eyes when the hypnotist's voice had not been heard for some time, or slip into a brief, relaxing sleep and then awaken normally. No one has ever disappeared for long— but we bet many would like to!

6. *Deep hypnosis is necessary for good results.*
    NOT TRUE. Any level of hypnosis, from light to very deep, can bring good results. You do not have to be "out" for hypnosis to be effective. In fact, you may just be in a highly mellow, relaxed, calm and peaceful state. One might describe the hypnotic state as "feeling as if your mind were floating above your physical body."

With the myths dispelled, let us continue.

Chapter 3: TurboCharged Mind Seeds...

◈ People fear hypnosis only because they do not understand it.

◈ Hypnosis will not weaken your mind or will.

◈ You will not violate your moral beliefs or lose your will while under hypnosis.

◈ An intelligent person is easier to hypnotize than a not-so-intelligent person.

◈ The conscious mind possesses a "critical faculty."

◈ The subconscious mind has a feedback mechanism.

◈ Self-hypnosis is a natural God-given power that everyone is born with.

4

Can I Benefit from Hypnosis?

With very few exceptions—usually psychotic or hysterical individuals—anyone can benefit from hypnosis. After all, as I explained before, hypnosis is a highly relaxed state—and who couldn't use a little more relaxation in their life?

While someone like you is in a relaxed, hypnotic state, a wide variety of suggestions can be introduced. For most people, if the hypnotic trance focuses on enhancing the way the individual views his/herself, great overall results can be achieved.

The key to successful hypnosis is lack of judgment. This is why we suggested in Chapter 1 that you "free your mind and the rest will follow." Just being open to new experiences is helpful, and is a logical step toward allowing your mind to be more free and receptive. During a hypnosis session, or a guided meditation or directed trance, if you are able to simply listen and avoid rationalizing or judging the suggestions being applied, the results can be quite remarkable. Interestingly, during a session with an experienced hypnotist (in person or by audio download), whether you judge or not becomes irrelevant—because the hypnotist will be able to assume you are judging and utilize techniques to work you through your judgment processes. A good session or recording clears the way by setting the stage with deep relaxation to eliminate the likelihood that you will stay in an exclusively conscious state. The result is that you are relaxed enough to cease being able to analyze what is occurring; instead, the unconscious mind begins the process of registering new and positively constructive ideas.

The subconscious mind is much like a computer. It has memory banks that store all our experiences. At the same time, like a computer, it is programmable—and as we discussed, this programming consists of our experiences and our thoughts about them. Most of us have left the programming of our subconscious "computers" up to the outside world. The result is that a substantial amount of what we think, feel, and do has been left to chance. Our "input" has been manipulated by our parents, friends, family, advertising, big business, laws, church and religious doctrine, unwritten social mores and our own undirected thoughts.

There is no doubt that all these factors have had a profound influence on how we consciously and unconsciously perceive ourselves and the world around us.

Through hypnosis, if you are willing to open your mind, you will reach new heights of greatness. You are the controlling factor. It is always through your own efforts that change occurs. Your receptivity to hypnosis, and any follow-up suggestions or guidelines, can make a subtle or dramatic difference in your lifestyle, success and feelings of wellbeing.

The following are just a few of the ways that hypnosis can be used to enhance your overall direction in life:

◈ *Image Enhancement/Self Esteem:* Hypnosis can be used to reprogram thinking to eliminate the reoccurrence of past negative behaviors, increase confidence and attain self-acceptance. New mental "trance-scripts" can be instilled for specific goals, and feelings of comfort can be included in the suggestions, leading to the achievement of subsequent success. When self-image is enhanced, most problems will take care of themselves.

❖ *Excess Fat Loss:* Hypnosis can be very effectively used to motivate fat loss, reprogram eating habits and help establish a healthful program for weight maintenance and a healthful lifestyle. Clinical trials have proven, that those who diet, particularly with a program like Turbo-Charged™, while also incorporating hypnosis can experience a 146% greater success.

❖ *Stress:* Using hypnosis, techniques to reduce or eliminate stress can be learned and integrated at the conscious and unconscious levels. Hypnosis promotes relaxation and is immensely useful for reprogramming specific behavior patterns, reactions and interpretations of stress or stressful situations.

❖ *Smoking*: Through creative self-enhancement imagery, an individual's smoking habit can be eliminated and a plan can be implemented for permanent behavior modification. Becoming a non-smoker is easy with a few good hypnosis sessions.

❖ *Creativity*: Hypnosis can release blocked potential in many areas, including writing, painting, speaking and performing. Since the imaginative and creative mind form the foundation of hypnosis, the process of guided meditation or trance can open anyone to recognizing talents that they might have been unaware of. The trance state will often add insights that were not available at the conscious level, while personal output and expression are enhanced.

These are just a few benefits. This book is about image enhancement on every level—along with a focus on getting you to believe that you can live your dreams, reach your goals and be lean for life while increasing your health and living in a truly awe-inspiring, TurboCharged body and mind.

So can hypnosis help you? Are there ways that you can benefit from its power? If you are receptive and ready to open your mind, the answer is yes. Absolutely yes!

Chapter 4: TurboCharged Mind Seeds...

◈ Everyone can benefit from hypnosis.

◈ Your subconscious mind is like a computer. It is ready to be directed to accept new positive programming.

◈ Self-hypnosis (which is what all hypnosis is) is a tool that will enable you to fully realize your potential in life.

◈ More is demanded of our mental powers today than ever before. Self-hypnosis is a powerful tool that can help meet this need.

◈ Hypnosis can revive the 92% of your mind that goes unused.

◈ Hypnosis can make positive contributions to every aspect of your life on the physical, mental and spiritual planes.

Chapter

5

Why You Feel How You Feel

I once read that we have been hypnotized every day of our lives. There was a time I didn't believe this. But today I certainly do.

We have all been hypnotized daily (except perhaps during our very early infant years). In fact, I'd argue that most people need to be de-hypnotized. Think about it: We wear the clothes that advertisements suggest; seek to drive cars that offer status as well as basic transportation; and wear perfumes and colognes that promise love (or sex), not just a scent. Having worked with clinical drug trials for almost 20 years, I've witnessed countless instances of the "placebo effect," whereby the patients in blind studies who do not receive any of the drug being tested nevertheless inexplicably get better. Of course there are important exceptions to my theory that everyone needs to be de-hypnotized—but there is also plenty to support it.

Suggestions from others are very potent. Your interpretation of these suggestions and your own subsequent thoughts are quite potent as well. For example, not only are you influenced by your conscious thoughts, like what you want to eat; your subconscious mind is a pretty powerful place, too, as it harbors old, unconsciously recorded desires for foods that you know aren't in your best diet or health interests, but that you somehow recall as a "reward" or "treat."

Your subconscious mind is constantly influencing your life by generating impulsive reactions and a continuous stream of thought. These impulses and thoughts can include likes, dislikes, fears, pre-formed opinions and judgments, ideas and physical actions. The thoughts can trigger strong emotional reactions that in retrospect might seem to be overreactions. Yet for some reason, at a given moment, it is as if a force is compelling you to act—or shall we say "re"-act? But the question is: What is it that is responsible for our re-action?

As another example, have you ever had a conversation that includes the line: "Why are you being so stubborn about _____?" The next statement might be: "You're not hearing a word that I'm saying." This is usually followed by: "It's just the way it is. That's just how I feel! This is who I am." Often, this kind of conversation is accompanied by behavior that we might admit is illogical. Furthermore, we might concede that our comments are often just weak rationalizations if we really desired to be intro-spective at all. When we respond emotionally, our subconscious thoughts are what spew forth. Once we start acting on emotions or from a subconscious state, listening to reason becomes nearly impossible—because our minds are flooded with excess baggage that we often don't even know we are carrying.

All of us are lugging around excess subconscious baggage. Yes, all of us. No exceptions. Making it more challenging is that subconscious thoughts can work in complete opposition to your conscious desires, thoughts and goals, negating any progress you attempt to make.

Are we doomed?

No. Luckily, each of us has a God-given ability to dump this unnecessary baggage and gain greater access to our subconscious desires, thoughts and goals—and to stop blocking our own progress.

To dump this baggage, you must gain access to your subconscious mind and reprogram your mental computer in a positive and constructive way. Your subconscious is waiting to be used and governed by you. It is very open to the idea of putting you back in control. If there are thoughts in your mind that are incongruous, your subconscious realizes this. But it needs some help getting its proverbial ducks back in a row. Your subconscious wants to allow you to decide what you think. Given the chance to act, which is triggered by hypnotic trance, it will make you figure out what you want to do in life…instead of letting your old program decide for you. We've all been dealt different hands in the game of life, some good and some downright unjust and crappy. However, it is how we play those hands that will affect the way we play the game. Our ultimate happiness and greater peace of mind represent the winning hand.

Chapter 5: *TurboCharged Mind Seeds...*

◈ All of us have been hypnotized every day of our lives.

◈ When we re-act, we are often acting from a subconscious memory.

◈ Impulses, likes and dislikes, as well as prejudiced feelings, are the result of subconscious programming from others and situations in our past.

◈ Advertisers know the powerful effects of hypnosis, particularly the hypnotic impact of television and commercial advertisements.

◈ Hypnosis is the perfect tool for reprogramming all the negative messages that are adversely affecting your life.

.

Chapter

6

What You Think Is What You Are

Your self-image is the key to your personality and your behavior. If you change your self-image, you change your personality and your behavior. If you change your personality and behavior, you will also change the people and circumstances you attract into your life experience.

More important than this is that your self-image sets the boundaries of your individual accomplishments. Your self-image becomes your definition of what you can and cannot do. If you enhance your self-image by building a sense of wellbeing—understanding that you are a loved, necessary, worthwhile individual—you can expand the "area of the possible." A new, improved self-image can turn failure into success by giving free rein to capabilities and talents that were dormant under the stress of all your excess mental and emotional baggage.

In his perennial bestseller *Psycho-Cybernetics*, Dr. Maxwell Maltz explained it this way: "Insofar as function is concerned, the brain and nervous system constitute a marvelous and complex 'goal striving mechanism,' a sort of built-in automatic guidance system which works for you as a 'success mechanism,' or against you as a 'failure mechanism,' depending on how YOU, the operator, operates it and the goals you set for it."

Your self-image is affected—for better or for worse—by experience. Intellect alone just doesn't cut it. You cannot rationalize your way through deeply imbedded emotional experiences that have been imprinted into your subconscious mind. Thus the exasperation behind the phrase "You aren't being rational!" that is often voiced in heated discussion within passionate relationships where something of value is perceived as being at stake.

Knowingly or not, your current self-image was forged by your collective experiences as a safety response. On some level, we build seemingly impenetrable walls to protect our "selves." At some point in the past, these protective mechanisms were quite valuable to us. However, this may not be the case anymore. The block (or blocks) that obstruct our ultimate happiness may not be serving the purpose they once did.

Let's look at love: It can't be taught. None of us can define it, despite attempts by thousands of books and poets. Rather, love is something that we have either experienced and felt or not. Comparably, whatever state you are in now, however you feel about yourself, your self-esteem and self-image are directly related to your experience rather than to what you have learned.

Real life can be a pretty ruthless teacher. If you have been told you are fat, ugly, stupid, a pain in the neck, worthless, or have been abused either physically or mentally in any way—all of which hold the potential of making you think you're pretty unlovable—there's a really good possibility that you believe it's true, and that your actions, appearance and life bespeak it. Whether you were criticized directly or not matters little. If you sensed any of this from another person who held any importance or influence in your life, your experiences and interpretation of those experiences can lead to some pretty seriously unproductive behavior(s).

Now we don't claim to have made any Earth-shattering revelations here. The revelation is this: With hypnosis, in a state of trance, using guided meditation, you can make the changes you want in your life the same way your problems started—via experience.

Right about now, you are probably thinking that this is crazy—but it's not! If your life experience has left you feeling less than wonderful and less worthy than others, all you need are some positive experiences! OK, now I'm sure you think I'm crazy. You are saying to yourself, "Yeah, right Dian—I'm just going to run out and get myself some supportive, happy, life experience—when I can't even look at myself in the mirror…"

This is where the power and wonderment of hypnosis comes in. Experimental and clinical psychologists have proven beyond a shadow of a doubt that the human nervous system cannot tell the difference between "actual" experience and an experience imagined vividly and in detail. Pretty cool, right? It sure is.

Simply, the idea behind hypnosis is this: First, create a deep relaxation state, and then utilize the power naturally contained within your imagination to achieve what you want in your life. Hypnosis provides the format for this creative visualization, thus enabling you to create what you truly want: love, fulfillment, enjoyment, satisfying relationships, rewarding work, self-expression, health, fat loss, beauty, prosperity, inner peace, harmony or whatever your heart desires. As Shakti Gawain wrote in *Creative Visualization*, "Thought is a quick, light, mobile form of energy. It manifests instantaneously, unlike the denser forms of matter."

Anytime we create something, we always do so first in thought form. A thought or idea always precedes manifestation. "I think I'll eat lunch" is the idea that precedes making a meal. "I want a new suit" precedes going out and buying one. An author first has an idea, then the book gets written. A trader first calculates an opinion of the market, then makes a trade. A teacher researches and contemplates a lesson, then educates others. The examples are as infinite as the thoughts themselves.

Ideas are like blueprints. What you think is what you'll build. Follow this concept through—the same principle holds true even if we do not take direct physical action to manifest and fulfill our ideas. Simply having an idea or thought, holding it in your mind, is energy. This energy will eventually actualize somehow into form or being. If you constantly think of illness, you will eventually become ill. If you believe you are a kind and lovable person, your actions will follow suit.

The basic universal law, "As you sow, so shall you reap" is at play here. From a practical standpoint, this means that you will always attract whatever you think about the most, believe in most strongly, expect on the deepest levels, and/or imagine most vividly.

If you are feeling negative, fearful, insecure, unworthy or anxious, you will tend to attract the very people, situations and experiences that you are seeking to avoid. However, the good part is that if you are basically a positive person with an up, cheery attitude, who expects and envisions pleasure, satisfaction and happiness, you will attract people and create situations and events that conform to your positive expectations. So the more positive energy and reinforcement you program into your mind— imagining who you really are and what you really want—the more positive events begin to manifest as realities in your life.

Chapter 6: TurboCharged Mind Seeds...

❖ Your self-image is the key to your personality and your behavior.

❖ If you change your self-image, you change your personality and your behavior.

❖ Your self-image sets the boundaries of your individual accomplishments, becoming your definition of what you can and cannot do.

❖ Self-hypnosis will enhance your self-image by steadily increasing your sense of wellbeing and understanding that you are a loved, necessary, worthwhile individual. Each time you listen to your chosen download(s), this effect will increase.

❖ Hypnosis can expand your mind into the "area of the possible."

❖ With hypnosis, your mind can be freed from excess mental and emotional baggage and create a new perspective that can realistically turn any failure into success.

❖ Thoughts are a form of energy. Ideas are blueprints. With hypnosis you can create new positive road maps that will lead to a happier, more satisfying and more productive life.

❖ The more positive energy and reinforcement you program into your mind with hypnosis and TurboCharged™ minutes of visualization, the more positive events begin to manifest as realities in your life.

7

Change through Visualization

The process of change does not occur on superficial levels, through mere "positive thinking," although positive thoughts on a daily basis are certainly worth practicing.

If you want to create a significant change in your life, it will require some work on your part. It involves exploring, discovering and changing your deepest, most basic attitudes toward life— although not necessarily consciously. Quite often, subconscious beliefs are not readily admitted to your conscious mind. There is too much internal conflict involved when we go against social mores or counter what we've been taught or learned to believe in order to protect ourselves on some deep level.

Beliefs that motivate us are seldom if ever expressed verbally. Likewise, the things we may say we believe consciously don't motivate us. For example, none of us really wants to live and eat in a way that sets the stage for obesity, diabetes, cancer, heart disease or any other serious and debilitating illness. None of us want to be stressed and work ourselves to death either. No one can be alive in this day and age and not know that smoking can cause cancer and premature death. Yet unconscious forces are clearly at work for many of us, exemplifying the conflict between what we say and do.

Subconscious beliefs result from countless factors. The repetition of certain ideas by parents, relatives, schoolteachers and friends can cause a variety of subconscious beliefs to develop. This starts early, with the desire to please parents and teachers while experiencing the least amount of disapproval or discomfort, and continues into our teen years as we all try to be "cool" and fit in. As we move into adulthood, not much changes as we seek to socialize with others who seem to hold beliefs similar to those we hold dear. Beliefs are also caused by inference, when any one of those aforementioned influencers in our lives might have said one thing, but demonstrated something entirely different with their lives and actions. A prime example of this is the neglectful or abusive parent who nevertheless tells their child they are loved. Subconscious beliefs can also be the result of traumatic experiences. Sexual abuse, for one, can manifest in any number of self-destructive ways, ranging from frigidity to overly promiscuous behavior to severe eating disorders.

Right about now, you are likely asking yourself, "What do I subconsciously believe? How can I know what I believe subconsciously that might be affecting my behavior in a less-than-positive way?" In seeking the answers, remember that subconscious belief affects your conscious behavior. Your subconscious feeds your mind with whatever it has uncritically accepted from the conscious mind. You might consciously tell yourself that you want to live a long, healthy life. But the fact is that you don't eat well or get active. Maybe you tell yourself you want to have a better love life or simply have more friends and be more social—yet you repeatedly do things that sabotage your relationships, while possibly blaming the breakup of the relationship on others. Your actions demonstrate that your subconscious is convinced you are inferior in some way in the area of your life that is causing you the most pain. The scope of this truth is unlimited. Here are the harsh realities: Men and women are failures, men and women are slaves to habit, many of us are emotional cripples—not because we consciously want to be, but because our subconscious minds have been convinced we have to be.

Although this might sound hopeless, it really isn't. We were not designed to be failures. Mechanisms exist to turn this around—in much the same way the problems began in the first place. With hypnosis and self-hypnosis, the subconscious can be reached and "spoken to," and "redirected, retrained and re-educated," to act in a more fruitful and rewarding way.

Through guided meditation and creative visualization, all hypnosis, which is always self-hypnosis, can initiate the process of deep, meaningful growth. In the process, you will circumvent the causes of your fears and negative attitudes that have been holding you back and blocking you from achieving your goals, greater satisfaction and deeper fulfillment in life. During a state of deep relaxation, a clear, more accurate picture can be formed, whereby you can see yourself the way you really are. Dissolving these limiting attitudes, you are well on your way to becoming whatever and whoever you want to be—loved, social, slim, healthy, stress-free, organized, vibrant. You can visualize and create a new life that has greater happiness, fulfillment, health and love.

As you keep reading, hopefully with that "free mind" we talked about in Chapter 1, we ask you to be careful not to get hung up on the notion of visualization. We've been talking a lot about that. Sometimes when people are introduced to the concept of change through hypnosis, they begin to worry that they are not or will not be able to actually "see" a mental image when they try to visualize. Some people say they see very clear, sharp images when they close their eyes and imagine something. Others, and I'm one of these, say they don't really "see" anything; they just sort of "think about it," or imagine what they are looking at, or

become aware of a feeling. Any of these works. It is not necessary to mentally "see" an image. We all use our imaginations in a
wide variety of ways, so whatever process you use to visualize is
just fine. Some of us are more visual. Some can imagine sounds
associated with an experience, and others simply "feel" it. We
each learn differently, and each way of learning is equally effective
and responsive to hypnosis meditations. As William James said,
"Our belief at the beginning of a doubtful undertaking is the one
thing that ensures the successful outcome of the venture." So for
now, just work on believing in the process of hypnosis and that
yes, change is possible, even for you.

So how do you start to visualize? It's easier than you might
think. After you read this paragraph, take a moment and practice
visualizing using the following suggestions.

Imagine biting hard into a very sour lemon. Imagine this now.
Notice anything? Is there a bit more saliva in your mouth than a
second ago? Is your mouth watering just a bit? This is the power
of visualization at work. For most of us, just thinking about biting
into a lemon will trigger uncontrolled, automatic salivation.

Now take your visualization talents a bit further and try
this:

Close your eyes and take a few deep breaths. Allow yourself
to breathe deeply and get very comfortable in the chair you are
in, or lay down on a couch or bed.

Now recall some pleasant experience you have had—an exciting first date, a delicious dinner with a friend, an enjoyable conversation, an award you received, getting a great massage, swimming
in cool water, making wonderfully passionate love. Remember the
experience as vividly as possible. Enjoy the pleasant sensations
once again. Relax and relish the feelings for a few minutes.

You should be able to just relax and enjoy the feelings, letting
your imagination roam freely.

If you are unable to visualize and feel like you "just can't do it," this is probably due to a fear of what you believe will be encountered by looking inside yourself. This fear, of unacknowledged feelings and / or emotions, is sometimes a block. But it is one that can be worked through with a little practice and repeated listening to a quality hypnosis recording. The truth is that there is nothing within you that can hurt you; it is only your fear of experiencing your own feelings that can keep you trapped. Your fears arise from things you don't confront. Once you are willing to look fully and deeply at the source of a fear, it loses its power.

Chapter 7: *TurboCharged Mind Seeds...*

❖ The process of change does not occur on superficial levels, through mere "positive thinking," although positive thoughts on a daily basis are certainly worth practicing.

❖ If you want to create a significant change in your life, it will require some work on your part. It involves exploring, discovering and changing your deepest, most basic attitudes toward life—although not necessarily consciously. Hypnosis makes this possible.

❖ Subconscious beliefs are not readily admitted to your conscious mind. There is too much internal conflict involved when we go against social mores and customs or counter what we've been taught or learned to believe, in order to protect ourselves on some deep level.

❖ Beliefs that motivate us are seldom, if ever, expressed verbally.

❖ God, or any other Creator that you might believe in, does not want us to be failures.

❖ The subconscious can be reached and "spoken to," or "redirected, retrained and re-educated," to act in a more fruitful and rewarding way via hypnosis and self-hypnosis.

❖ All hypnosis, which is always self-hypnosis, can initiate the process of deep meaningful growth through guided meditation and creative visualization.

❖ Hypnosis allows your mind to circumvent the causes of the fears and negative attitudes that have been holding you back and blocking you from achieving your goals, greater satisfaction and deeper fulfillment in life.

❖ During hypnosis, a state of deep relaxation is achieved. This relaxation allows your mind to reconcile issues by dissolving limiting attitudes.

◈ Everyone experiences hypnosis differently: Some actually see a picture when they visualize; others "feel" the experience. Some people also bring in other senses like taste, smell and hearing.

◈ Self-hypnosis will put you on your way to becoming whatever and whoever you want to be—loved, social, lean, strong, healthy, stress-free, organized and vibrant. With hypnosis, you can visualize and create a new life that has greater happiness, fulfillment, health and love.

Chapter

8

Understanding Subconscious Motives

You might think that everyone reading this book is doing so for different reasons. Actually, this isn't true. How I see it is this: We are each looking for our acceptable self. We all need that wholesome self-esteem that enables us to trust and believe in ourselves. We all want to be free to verbally, visually and creatively express ourselves and our thoughts, rather than stifle ourselves, hide or suppress our feelings and emotions.

When your self-image is intact and secure, you are ready for almost anything, and bursting with enthusiasm and energy. You are confident and you feel free to express yourself. You are willing to work and move through the insecurities that we all experience and forge ahead regardless of your discomfort, knowing that you'll survive and most likely ultimately thrive for having boldly ventured forth. When your self-image is shrouded in shame, guilt, or feelings of worthlessness, you revert into various hiding and self-shielding modes. Your creative expression is overridden and blocked. You find it difficult to speak, relate, act and sometimes function even at the most basic levels.

There are many good books that delve into the psychological reasons that people use food for comfort or punishment, and how this can lead to obesity, bulimia or anorexia. The bottom line is that people eat and gain excess body fat for a variety of reasons. People decide to lose their excess body fat for just as many reasons. The reasons you overeat may not be clear to you. Some are blatantly obvious—like being unable to resist a chocolate double hot fudge ice cream sundae with extra whipped cream that makes your mouth water even though you just finished a meal and are "full"—and some are not so obvious. It's the not-so-obvious reasons that we're concerned with in these pages.

Any motive that causes you long-term physical, emotional, social or mental discomfort is one that has most likely been buried in an attempt to avoid being identified. Finding the reason may not be as difficult as you might think. We have only identified a few common causes—apart from those related to serious illness—that explain why any of us chooses to overeat or, frankly, do anything that is counter-productive to our health and longevity. Let's look at the most typical:

Eating to Self-Reward. This is a biggie because the notion of "reward treats" has been ingrained in each of us since the beginning of our lives. As children we are told, "Eat up and you'll get dessert." "Behave and you'll get ice cream." "Use the toilet instead of a diaper and I'll give you a lollipop." As we get older, not much changes. If you get a promotion at work, it's usually associated with a company dinner. Food is held out as a reward. If you are out to dinner and opt for a low-calorie meal or choose to skip dessert, invariably you are asked, "Why are you depriving yourself?"

Through hypnosis and creative visualization, you can learn to go to any food-focused function, eat wisely, and still enjoy being there. You can learn new, more healthful and positive ways to reward yourself.

Eating to Entertain Yourself. This is similar in many ways to reward eating, but is grounded in a different motivation. Entertainment eating is what we are doing when we eat instead of reading a good book, taking a brief nap, enjoying a conversation with a friend, or taking a walk in some fresh air. Eating is a common strategy for killing time or abolishing boredom. Hypnosis and creative visualization can help inspire productive activities to prevent a binge and to utilize your time much better.

Eating to Forget an Unpleasant Experience. This is a pattern also established in childhood. A well-intentioned parent often soothes a crying child who has just scraped their knee by offering the child a cookie. As adults, we pig out to distract ourselves when the guy or girl of our dreams isn't quite enthusiastic about a second date. We indulge ourselves if we don't get the sale we need at work or if we fail to get the job we wanted. To assuage our feelings, we seek comfort from the refrigerator, pastry shop, and ice cream parlor. But really, how long does that banana cream pie really stave off our feelings of sadness? Not very long. In fact, often we don't even notice or enjoy the junk we are eating in an effort to feel better, since we are not "in the moment" enough to experience taste; rather, we are simply "stuffing emotions." Hypnosis and creative visualization enable you to imagine how long you'll be wearing that pecan pie—allowing your rational self to take over and direct you into a more positive direction.

Failure to Recognize Consequences. There are very few people who don't like the taste of candy, cakes, pies, doughnuts, bread or French fries. However, eating them—in spite of the scale going up and a doctor's warnings about rising blood pressure, diabetes, cancer and other illnesses—results from ignoring that our diet has a direct effect on our health. With self-hypnosis, you can bridge the gap that exists in these situations and begin to "eat to live."

Eating When You Need Love. This is a difficult one to try on. It hurts to admit that you need love, and it hurts to admit you eat to compensate for its absence. Now, if you try to understand where this comes from, it really isn't so traumatic. Back to childhood again: Most of us, if we were lucky, didn't just get a bottle when we cried; we got picked up and held. The power of touch should never be underestimated. Often we eat when we really need a hug, or wish someone would tell us that they love us just the way we are. When we don't get this love—because we're afraid to ask for it—we give ourselves love in the form of the delicious, forbidden, empty-calorie foods we think we love to eat. There's only one problem with this behavior: As we get bigger and fatter, we sometimes view ourselves as less lovable—and a vicious cycle is born.

Hypnosis and creative visualization provide reinforcement and positive feelings of self-worth and love.

Eating Because You Are Afraid of Sex. Of what? S-E-X. If you believe you are unattractive to potential partners, you don't have to worry about the consequences of a relationship. You don't have to worry about whether you'll get a call for a second date, because you have used food to insulate yourself from these potentially uncomfortable feelings. Of course there are interesting, talented, overweight people who still have sex appeal—but the general rule is that if you are not receptive, you do nothing to make yourself appear enticing; you "bury" your attractive self.

Hypnosis and creative visualization can help to enhance your self-image and your right to experience all aspects of your personality, including your sexuality.

Eating Because You Are Generally Afraid. This covers a broad base. Perhaps you eat because being overweight allows you to rationalize your failure to do the things you're afraid of doing. Perhaps being fat allows you to blame your failure to get that promotion on discrimination linked to your appearance. Maybe the pretty girl who wants to be an actress or model eats because she can stall the rejection she anticipates: "Before I go out on another audition, I'll have to lose a few pounds." If you really want to be a baseball player but think you won't make the team, it is easier to eat and gain a few pounds: At least this way you'll never have to deal with the possibility of getting cut from the team.

Maybe you're afraid of your health. Some of us have been raised to feel that being thin is a sign of sickness. You may believe that you have to "eat up" for energy.

Maybe you eat because you fear your relationship with your spouse is falling apart, and it's easier to deal with the situation by eating—and insulating your disillusionment with fat.

Maybe your spouse is encouraging you to eat during your moments of dieting weakness, because your obesity is their insurance against competition from other males or females. Maybe your spouse is sabotaging your dieting efforts, because they are afraid that if you shape up, they might need to take a good look at themselves.

The fear factor is endless. If you take the time, you can figure out just what is immobilizing you. Once your fear(s) is isolated, hypnosis and creative visualization will fortify the changes in thinking needed to overcome them.

Did you recognize any patterns? I know this is uncomfortable, but it is a worthwhile process nonetheless if you are going to actualize yourself into the person you know you really are.

Your initial determination of why you overeat or indulge in any other negative practice or behavior is valuable and can provide good information about your psyche. But interestingly, knowing "why" is not essential to your success when you use hypnosis to obtain a healthier and leaner body or to change any other behavior. The procedure you'll follow is the same. You must replace the emotional satisfaction that you are deriving from the action you want to change with an activity that serves the same purpose. For example, if you are eating when you are tired, maybe you really need a nap or brief meditation instead. If you are eating when you're feeling stressed, maybe a walk around the block or some other physical activity is in order. You need to determine an appealing and satisfying alternative to food. Notice I said "appealing and satisfying." I am not suggesting that you go wash your car or clean your apartment whenever you're hungry—but as you know, one of the TurboCharged™ steps is to get up and get active if you are hungry and about to eat. Do something fun that you enjoy. Take a nap that relaxes you. Go to the park and read a book. Take the dog for a walk. Get up and at 'em.

Hypnosis and self-hypnosis or creative visualization will serve you by reinforcing your new, more productive behaviors.

Now It's Your Turn.

1. *Determine where/when you eat (*or do any other counter-productive behavior): in bed, in front of the TV, in the car, at your desk, etc.* _____

_____

2. *Determine your eating patterns or the "why" triggering your eating (*or any other counter-productive behavior):*
   ◈ I eat* when I want to reward myself.
   ◈ I eat* to entertain myself.
   ◈ I eat* when I need to forget an unpleasant experience.
   ◈ I eat* when I need love.
   ◈ I eat* because I am afraid of intimacy with the opposite sex.
   ◈ I eat* because I am afraid that _____

   _____

   _____

❖ I eat*_____

_____

_____

3. *Now determine an appealing and satisfying alternative to food.** *Give yourself a few suggestions. For example:*

❖ When I want to reward myself, I take a walk or do a minute workout to stress my muscles, because I will feel extra good about myself and my achievement.

❖ When I need love, I will call my friends and family and ask for assurance and support.

❖ When I am bored, I will take the time to read a good book or get out and go to a movie.

Identify your behavior and think of something more constructive you can do.

_____

_____

_____

_____

_____

_____

Chapter 8: TurboCharged Mind Seeds...

◈ We are each looking for our acceptable self.

◈ We all need that wholesome self-esteem that enables us to trust and believe in ourselves and the choices we make.

◈ Each of us desires to feel the freedom to verbally, visually and creatively express ourselves and our thoughts. We are conflicted and less happy when we stifle ourselves, hide or suppress our feelings and emotions.

◈ When your self-image is shrouded in shame, guilt, or feelings of worthlessness, you revert into various hiding and self-shielding modes. Your creative expression is overridden and blocked. You find it difficult to speak, relate, act and sometimes function even at the most basic levels.

◈ When your self-image is intact and secure, you are ready for almost anything, and bursting with enthusiasm and energy. You are confident and you feel free to express yourself. You are willing to work and move through the insecurities that we all experience and forge ahead regardless of your discomfort, knowing that you'll survive and most likely ultimately thrive for having boldly ventured forth.

◈ Negative and excessive emotions are enemies that cannot be combated with food.*

◈ Excessive guilt can do great harm and is often assuaged with food.*

◈ False guilt can ruin your life. Hypnosis is very effective at removing false guilt.

◈ You may suffer from the sins of your fathers, but you are not responsible for them.

❖ People who don't trust themselves were somehow taught not to trust themselves. This lesson can be unlearned with hypnosis.

❖ Through hypnosis, you can change your attitude toward the past, which will determine your attitude toward the future. More so, you can learn to trust yourself and your ability to make healthy choices.

❖ With hypnosis, you can be reconditioned to accept success when it comes your way.

❖ Hypnosis can help your conscious and subconscious mind replace food "rewards" with others that are more constructive and likely to help you reach your goal of a lean and healthy TurboCharged body.

❖ There are three things you can do to cope constructively with bad past experiences:

1. *Leave them in the past. Forget bitterness. Be kind to yourself. Don't blame the past.*

2. *Learn from past experiences.*

3. *Laugh at them.*

❖ Five things you can do with good past experiences are:

1. *Build upon them for greater success.*

2. *Use them as inspiration.*

3. *Use them as a life instruction manual.*

4. *Keep them in the front of your mind to sustain your spirit in times of need.*

5. *Use your faith to increase your confidence in the future.*

❖ Remember: Tomorrow is yours to use any way you want. Taking one step at a time, you can make choices that provide greater satisfaction, rewards, health and happiness.

Steps for Effective Hypnosis & Dynamic Creative Visualization

Earlier, we dealt with prevalent misconceptions regarding hypnosis. Now let's review the facts.

All hypnosis is self-hypnosis. Whatever a hypnosis or guided-meditation session can do for you, you can do for yourself if you take the time to understand how hypnosis works.

Hypnosis is a normal and natural state, and as I've mentioned before, you have been hypnotized with or without your awareness every day of your life. Anytime you have been so engrossed in something that you were unaware of your surroundings, you were in a state of hypnosis.

Hypnosis is an altered state of consciousness. It is also a state of hypersuggestibility. When you are hypnotized, you are conscious, but your consciousness is limited to the suggestions you are receiving—assuming they will benefit you in some positive way. There are degrees of consciousness. The consciousness you are experiencing right now as you read these words is different from the consciousness you might have felt when you woke up or took a shower this morning. For most people, it takes an hour to become fully awake and begin functioning at maximum capacity. Yet when you wake up, you are certainly conscious—just maybe not as conscious as you might be at other times during your day. If you were walking along the street and a car started veering in your direction, you would become very conscious. Your whole body would get involved in the process as your brain, nervous system, heart, glands and muscles would spring into action to prevent your injury or death. Conscious states vary in degree and depth.

When you are in a hypnotic state, your attention is narrowed to the thought or idea being given to you at that moment. Hypnosis is experiencing consciousness at its highest level. In a normal state of consciousness, you are aware of many things, including noise, people, smells and more. Under hypnosis, you are totally aware— but of only one thing. You might hear noises, conversations or other sounds, but they seem to drift way into the background. Instead, your mind is riveted to the one thing—the suggestion you are giving yourself or choosing to receive that will help adjust whatever your conscious and / or subconscious mind instinctively knows is out of balance.

Hypnosis is a state we are always in to one degree or another; but our suggestibility is increased in a hypnosis session or while listening to one of the TurboCharged meditation downloads. To appreciate this, recall how, when someone yawns, it seems to be contagious. Or how, when someone clears their throat, you might find yourself doing the same thing. Ever see a TV commercial for food and suddenly get the urge to eat? Why do I point all this out? Don't ever believe that you aren't suggestible. You can benefit from hypnosis. You've already been hypnotized count-less times. Now you are learning how to use this power for your own selfish benefit. And for the record, this kind of selfishness is a very good thing.

When you begin to formulate your new "programming" thoughts, always use positive reinforcement and replacement rather than negatives. For instance, to relieve tension, you should say "I am relaxing" rather than "I am not tense." (This is because the use of negative terms, like "tense," will keep your subconscious focused on them unnecessarily.) If you say "I am relaxing," the "negative" tension is displaced. A state of tension cannot coexist with a state of relaxation. Another example would be "I am a non-smoker" instead of "I don't smoke." The first is a statement of what you want to be; the second forces you to think of smoking first before negating it. Each time you change your mental programming by replacing a problem with a positive counterpart, you defeat a negative without fighting it. By ignoring the negative's existence, you keep from feeding the negative thoughts within your subconscious.

If you have determined that you eat when you are lonely, your hypnosis script or creative visualization should be positively oriented. In other words, do not say "When I am lonely, I will not eat." Rather, reinforce the changes you are going to make to alter the pattern: "If I feel lonely, I am going to call a friend, participate in volunteer work, write a letter or go visit a neighbor." Whatever substitute behavior you choose is fine as long as you make it positive and something you really would enjoy doing.

Let's review some of the basic steps that are necessary for effective hypnosis and creative visualization.

1. *Set a goal.*

   Decide what you would like to have, work toward, be, realize or create. It can be anything: a new awe-inspiring, healthy and fat-free body; a better relationship; a change in a behavior that is hindering relationships; increased prosperity; a more peaceful mind; better physical condition; or whatever. Choose a goal that that will enable you to maximize your feelings of success as you actively apply your imagination.

2. *Create a clear picture or idea.*
    Make a mental picture about whatever goal you chose. If you can't "see" the goal, feel it. Think of it exactly the way you want. Bring in as many senses as possible to imagine your goal. No matter what you choose, you should already think of it in the present tense. It already exists. Picture yourself within the situation with as many details as possible, again using as many of your senses to complete the vision.

3. *Focus on your picture or idea often.*
    Allow yourself as many moments as possible during the day to clear your mind and focus on your new image. Don't tell me you don't have time. This is important and only takes a few minutes. If you need to get away and have some peace, sit on the toilet a minute longer and allow your imagination to flow. (We knew we'd find a free minute in your busy schedule!) The more you think about it, the more it becomes integrated into your life. Focus on your goal in a clear yet gentle way. No excessive energy is necessary. Just clear, relaxed, soothing thought.

4. *Give your focus positive energy.*
    Use affirmations to keep your goal in focus. To affirm means to "make firm." Affirmations are strong, positive statements that something is already so. This isn't lying to yourself. It is mind talk that simply utilizes the principle: What you believe, is what is.

An affirmation can be any general or specific positive statement. Here are a few ideas:

◈   Every day in every way I'm getting better and better.

- ❖ Everything is coming to me easily and effortlessly.

- ❖ I am a radiant person filled with love.

- ❖ I am the master of my life.

- ❖ Everything I need is already within me.

- ❖ Perfect wisdom is in my heart.

- ❖ I am whole and complete in myself.

- ❖ I love and appreciate myself just as I am. I love to love and be loved.

- ❖ I am now attracting loving, satisfying, happy relationships into my life.

- ❖ I am getting leaner, healthier and more beautiful/handsome daily.

- ❖ I choose only healthy foods that keep me TurboCharged.

- ❖ I eat moderate portions and I stop when I am full.

- ❖ I am active every day and make my body stronger and more healthful.

- ❖ Greasy fried foods are like poison to my emotions and body.

- ❖ When I am full I push food away, take a big drink of water and get up from the table.

- ❖ I enjoy cool, refreshing, crisp fruits and vegetables.

- ❖ My body is leaner, more shapely and firmer every day.

- ❖ I look and feel great.

- ❖ I am relaxed and at peace. I eat only when I am truly hungry.

- ❖ I fill my tank with water before eating, then I eat if I am truly still hungry.

◈ I work the TurboCharged steps every day and I'm rewarded with a lean, healthy, awe-inspiring physique.

◈ I now have a perfect, satisfying, well-paying job.

◈ I always communicate clearly and effectively.

◈ I now have enough time, energy, wisdom, and money to accomplish all of my desires.

◈ It's okay for me to have everything I want.

◈ Infinite riches are now freely flowing into my life.

Now that you have some positive affirmations, let's take a look at how you can begin to implement them through self-hypnosis or creative visualization.

Steps for Self-Hypnosis or Creative Visualization

Stand up and take a nice big stretch. Reach for the sky as far as you can with both arms overhead, and step up on your toes. Really reach. Then slowly bend over from the waist and reach for your toes. Hold a minute and then slowly come up. Very slowly and easily, roll your neck a few times to the right and then to the left. Stretch again. Now sit or lie down in a comfortable position. Focus your attention on a specific spot either on the ceiling or on a wall directly in front of you. As you focus on your chosen spot, mentally say "relaxing" three times as you exhale. Then close your eyes.

Keeping your eyes closed, take another deep breath. As you exhale, count down your breaths from the number 10 all the way to the number one. Now imagine a relaxation force emanating from your eyes and flowing out all over your body like a blanket of soothing, warm, gentle air—going all the way down to your toes. Start with the top of your head. Imagine the relaxation wave flowing through your scalp, down into your forehead, across your face, into your jaw, down your neck. Then across your shoulders, down your arms, into your forearms, hands, all the way to your fingertips. Imagine a wave of relaxation going deep into your chest, your solar plexus, abdomen—making each breath into your lungs more and more relaxing. Then feel the wave of relaxation move into your hips, your bottom, your groin, and into your legs, thighs, calves, all the way down into your feet and toes.

Then count backward slowly again from 10 to one. Imagine you are descending a stairway. As you count down each number, you are going down, going deeper. Tell yourself that you are getting more and more relaxed with each breath and step.

When you reach the number one, give yourself this suggestion and follow it with your personal affirmation:

I am relaxed and calm.

(Now, your affirmation…)

After you repeat your personal affirmation three or four times, picture the same spot in your mind that you originally looked at. Imagine the spot moving all the way to the back of your head—taking your affirmation with it. Then forget the affirmation; just allow your inner mind to absorb it.

Then count from one to five, take some very deep breaths and allow yourself to open your eyes.

I would be remiss at this point if I didn't mention the invaluable benefits to be gained by consulting a professional hypnotherapist or purchasing some professionally recorded directive meditation downloads of your choice. A professional hypnotherapist is trained in technique and creative visualization. Experience and training enable a professional hypnotherapist to create effective, detailed imagery. The imagery is specifically designed for you to address your personal goals. The effectiveness of the hypnotic program is enhanced by the knowledgeable hypnotherapist who offers to provide a recording of the session. The recording becomes a powerful tailored tool. It is used to reaffirm the exacting individualized imagery and post-hypnotic suggestions designed with your specific needs in mind.

If you want to achieve optimum results from hypnotherapy, it is highly recommended that you plan a series of sessions and listen to your recorded download whenever you can. Each session will build a sound foundation for your subsequent self-hypnosis and creative visualization imagery. A series of sessions will help you understand motivation and technique while reinforcing your new goals—empowering you for effective, permanent change. The additional benefits of the TurboCharged download meditations as opposed to sessions with a hypnotherapist are constant reinforcement, cost, ease of use, time and place.

Chapter 9: TurboCharged Mind Seeds...

◈ Self-hypnosis is a totally natural experience that will enable you to realize your full potential in life.

◈ The proof of hypnosis is the positive post-hypnosis responses.

◈ Daily guided hypnosis sessions, like the TurboCharged Hypnosis Series of downloads, will create the best results when coupled with three to five one-minute visualizations throughout the day.

◈ All hypnosis is self-hypnosis.

◈ Subconscious beliefs feed into your conscious life and determine your behavior patterns.

◈ You can determine what you believe subconsciously by analyzing and taking an inventory of your conscious behavior.

◈ During hypnosis, your mind is relaxed and ready to accept positive suggestions that will affect your life for the better.

◈ When your subconscious becomes convinced of a fact, it colors your reality.

◈ Self-hypnosis, particularly directed hypnosis, is absolutely the best and easiest way to effect beneficial changes in your life.

Chapter

10

Assessing Your Determination

Earlier, we talked a bit about how we come to lack belief in ourselves and to distrust our thoughts and desires. I'd like to remind you that no normal person is born this way. An infant has innate self-trust, or else they would never risk crawling or walking. Anyone who has observed a child learning to stand typically marvels at the fact that the child is undeterred by the number of times they fall down. Children trust they can and will walk, and they don't quit. This confidence is a natural birthright. Any lack of self-trust or self-confidence is a learned behavior. It comes from statements like: "You are not as good as others at that, so don't even try." "Don't risk that; you can't do it." "It can't be done; why are you bothering to try?" "Don't do that! You'll get hurt." "We grow kids big in our family. We'll always be big. Accept it." Recalling an exact expression is irrelevant. What is relevant is the impression—the feelings that impacted our young and impressionable minds as we heard or observed others.

When any adult, particularly a parent, prevents a child from completing an age-appropriate task on their own, they are sending a message that says, "I don't believe in you. You need me to do this for you because you are not capable." Such a message can be conveyed when, for example, a parent buys their child sneakers with Velcro straps instead of laces because the parent "doesn't want to have to be tying the sneakers all the time." The fact is, all children are perfectly capable of learning how to tie their own shoes.

Such parents don't realize they are undermining their children's self-esteem and self-confidence. Yet the question will occur to the child regardless: If my parents don't believe in me, how can I believe in myself? We need to be challenged with age-appropriate tasks. As we work to accomplish anything, it becomes clear that we can "fall down and get up again." Each challenge keeps natural self-trust intact and growing.

You may lack self-confidence and question your ability to accomplish a goal. But here's where the power of hypnosis lies: You can change the present and future! You can rewrite the script. You can believe in yourself. There are absolutely no good reasons why you shouldn't believe in yourself. Not one! Excuses, maybe; but not a good reason. Excuses like: "I've tried before." "I've never had success with this." "Nothing goes right for me." The list could go on and on. But let's not confuse an excuse for a reason. There is no reason that you cannot succeed and reach your goal of a lean, healthy, awe-inspiring TurboCharged body or whatever else you decide you want today.

Just as we learn things, we can unlearn them.

Let's take a look at five reasons why you can, should and will believe in and trust yourself. These are adapted from the book, *The New Self-Hypnosis* by Paul Adams.

1. *You were born with self-confidence.*
   Remember the baby example? Yes, you were born helpless and needed an adult to fulfill your basic needs, but you were not afraid to do the things you could do, and

you didn't worry about what you couldn't do. A degree of competence is helpful when you want to accomplish something. However, competence does not equal confidence. There are many talented, competent people who lack confidence in their ability to excel in their field. If you find yourself working under someone who knows far less than you, it is likely due to your difference in degree of confidence. You don't have to be the smartest to be the boss; more often than not, confidence is the key factor.

There will be things you won't do well, and you will hire others to help fill certain roles—dentists, doctors, dry cleaners, plumbers, masons, mechanics...the list is endless. Some things you will do well; others not. Self-confidence is a state of believing that your best will be good enough and rewarding to you in whatever it is you desire to accomplish.

2. *Believe in yourself because God loves you and believes in you.*
   Don't doubt this. Just believe it, because it makes perfect sense for you to believe in yourself as God believes in you. There is a divine purpose for your existence; it is your responsibility to discover that purpose.

3. *Believe in yourself because others believe in you.*
   Disagree? I can assure you, no matter how many times you have failed or fallen short of your goals, there is someone who believes in you. I don't know if your cheering squad comes from your significant other, your children, your boss, a neighbor, an unrelated child or merely someone you have helped. If you still think I'm wrong, volunteer for a bit with some organization that helps orphaned children, the disabled or the homeless. Someone needs you and believes in you. Find them, keep them close and don't let them down.

4. *Believe in yourself because you have a responsibility in life to develop your talents and fulfill your goals.*

    Being unaware of or underestimating your talents and gifts is a common problem. You have at least one unique talent. It is not bravado or braggadocio to recognize a talent and do everything you can do to make everyone aware of your special ability. Average people are afraid to try, afraid to risk adventure and the unknown; and as a result, they are never discovered. Average is not the status quo. Each of us owes it to ourselves and to our Creator to acknowledge our talents and do whatever is in our power to develop and make those talents shine.

5. *Believe in yourself because you owe it to yourself.*

    If you lack self-confidence, you likely possess a large degree of self-consciousness, ego and self-centeredness. Sorry to be so harsh, but each of these is the enemy of self-confidence. If you find yourself thinking too much about yourself or worrying too much about what others are thinking about you, you are lacking self-confidence and missing out on a great deal of the good moments in life.

    Being overly concerned about what others are thinking about you is a form of self-flattery. Most people couldn't care less about what you are wearing or driving. People will like you, not because of what you have, but rather because they believe you are genuine. Likeable people are natural people. Self-confident people are natural people. When you start believing in yourself, you will stop thinking so much about yourself. When you say something that you wish you hadn't, you'll make amends if necessary and allow yourself to move on. Being self-confident is not being perfect. It is knowing that whatever you do, you give it your best shot. Perfection is not part of the definition. Remember, you owe it to yourself to believe in yourself, because when you do, belief from others will increase as well. As a final thought, don't worry about becoming overconfident. Just focus on approaching anything you want to do positively, keep a believing attitude, and assess the facts realistically—while bringing a boatload of gumption to act. The plumbers and the mechanics of the world don't ever have to worry about me taking their business. Their skills don't match my skill set, although every time my toilet is clogged or my car won't start I wish they did! None of us will ever be good at everything, but this shouldn't keep you from trying.

Now, let's take a look at the role intention plays in getting you on the road to change and greater self-confidence.

Intention is defined in the dictionary as "a determination to act in a certain way." Three things sum up your intention.

1. *Your Desire.*

   If you have a true desire to create that which you visualize—a strong, clear vision of purpose—you will achieve your goal. You must ask your heart if you really want your goal to be achieved. You must be willing to ask, "What more must I do to accomplish my goal?"

2. *Your Belief.*

   As I quoted before, "Your belief at the beginning of a doubtful undertaking is the one thing that ensures the successful outcome of the venture." The more you believe in your goal and the reality of attaining it, the more certain it will be that you succeed. You must believe with all your heart that you can reach your goal. As we just outlined, there are at least five good reasons for exercising your belief in yourself and your ability to reach your goal.

3. *Your Acceptance.*

Many of us like the idea of pursuing more than the actual catch. Sometimes what we think we want isn't really what we want at all. Our initial motivation may have been incorrect, and therefore what we think we want may not really be so. Let's say you wanted to lose your excess body fat because you believed it would make you more attractive to some guy or gal you were crazy about. So you diet a bit, ultimately get that date, but don't have such a great time—or maybe realize the individual you're fixated on really isn't your inspiration after all. This disillusionment could lead to a dieting slip and a binge, because the motivation to get lean and healthy in the first place was all wrong. Don't get in shape or commit to any other goal for anyone other than yourself. Believe me, the rest will fall right into place if it's meant to be.

Often, people attempt to live their lives backward: They try to amass more possessions, or more money, in order to do or get more of what they want, so that they will be happier.

The way it actually works is the reverse. You must first be who you really are, then do what you need to do, in order to have what you want. Then you'll be delighted to find everything else falling into place—maybe, although not necessarily, exactly as you pictured it.

Chapter 10: TurboCharged Mind Seeds...

- ◈ You were naturally born with self-confidence. Confidence is your birthright.

- ◈ Children trust they can and will walk, and they don't quit.

- ◈ Any lack of self-trust or self-confidence is a learned behavior.

- ◈ There are at least five important reasons to trust yourself.

- ◈ Intention = Determination.

- ◈ Desire + Belief + Acceptance = Your Intention and Determination.

- ◈ The power of hypnosis lies in the indisputable fact that you can change the present and future! You can rewrite any script to your ultimate benefit and reward.

Chapter

11

The Mind-Heart-Body Connection

Through our roles of funding and creating greater awareness for healthcare, biotechnology and pharmaceutical companies during the past 16 plus years, we have had the opportunity to work with some particularly brilliant minds on medical and scientific management teams at corporate, university and hospital levels. All of these doctors, scientists, researchers and corporate officers wake up every day and spend a tremendous amount of time and energy in hopes of finding a cure for the modern day diseases that are shortening the quality and lengths of our lives. Their primary focus is combating bodily invaders that steal our health and enter our bodies in the forms of virulent viruses, countless strains of bacteria, and an assortment of environmental toxins. The determination of these men and women to find cures and to prevent the devastating impact of these diseases is noble.

In modern medicine, most education, training and research centers on external factors, consequently the majority of research and drug development is focused on finding "cures" once a disease develops. The impact of nutrition, diet, lifestyle, activity, thoughts and emotions and their immense power to effect physical change rarely enters the curing equation and for the most part are overlooked or ignored. With the exception of a few very notable pioneers, there is a distinct and pervasive body/mind split in medicine and research today. This is particularly interesting considering the "placebo effect" discussed earlier, whereby these very same brilliant researchers regularly encounter the fact that when clinical trial patients "believe" they are being given a medicine that can cure them, they often have a comparable response (and sometimes even greater as in the case of a failed therapeutic) than with the real chemical entity being tested.

When legendary co-founder and chief genius of Apple Computers, Steve Jobs died prematurely at a mere 56 years old, articles generated from all kinds of sources were quick to point out that he took a non-traditional route to dealing with his illness. The medical establishment claimed that he cut his life short by opting out of surgery and chemotherapy, by his belief that good nutritious eating and meditation and relaxation would cure his cancer. Now considering the speed and intensity that defined Jobs' personality, and the fact that he apparently worked almost right up until the day he died, makes the relaxation component of his therapy doubtful. However, Dean Ornish, MD, a respected medical professional vouched for the fact that he did follow and make many dietary improvements. Hindsight in this case is not very insightful. We will never really know which approach -- traditional medicine or dietary and meditation measures --would have extended Mr. Jobs life for longer than he actually lived after his original diagnosis. Either perspective can only provide fodder for pure speculation and conjecture.

Regardless of the consensus, for the rest of us, it is foolish to deny the facts. Fried, processed, fatty, sugar-laden junk foods will not build healthy bodies for anyone and a healthy body is a requirement for a healthy mind. The two cannot be separated. Further, the reality is that the impact of our thoughts and daily stresses on our physical being are potentially just as deadly if left to run amuck on their own accord as is poor diet and lack of activity.

Our illnesses today are not simply bacterial, viral or chemical toxicity based. We suggest that you can control your health destiny more than you might believe; that the relationship between our thoughts and emotions along with the foods we consume for the greater part of our daily diet and the ways we choose to exercise and move our bodies, play a significant role in our health, wellbeing and our ultimate prospects for a long life. Although we would never tell anyone facing a debilitating disease that surgery, drugs and/or therapeutics have no benefit, as this is and always will be a very personal decision, we will propose that we need to get back to humanizing the cause and basis of the specific physical manifestations of obesity or any other subsequent dis-ease. We cannot lose sight of the impact of both thought and action on the whole person. As Doc Childre, the stress researcher and author of the groundbreaking HeartMath Solution Program pointed out, we all make unconscious statements that validate these connections. We say things like: "The stress of --- is killing me." "I think I'm going to have a heart attack if things keep up at this pace." "My heart is breaking with sadness." "I knew in my heart it was the wrong decision." In elaborating, Childre states: "Health is a delicate balance of rhythm, while dis-ease results from dis-rhythm. In a time where chaos and disrhythm are part of every day life, it's essential that we develop (mental) exercises (and healthful eating habits, Authors' notes) that help reestablish and regulate normal rhythms and thus promote health." From Childre's perspective, according to a forward written by Stephan Rechtschaffen, MD, "The heart is at the core of the body and at the core of how we think and feel. The 'solution' is derived from realizing that the heart is a physical object, a rhythmic organ and love itself. (We need to) recognize the heart as the central rhythmic force in the body and (as it) shows us how to use the coherent power of love to manage our thoughts and emotions. Like a pebble that creates a ripple of waves when dropped into a still pond, so love and positive feelings create a rhythm that spreads health and wellbeing throughout the body. In modern medicine, this is difficult to understand, because of our tendency to separate and differentiate mind and matter, emotions and the physical body, instead of recognizing the interconnection between them."

The mind and body are connected via an intricate electrical system. Yet, the intertwined connection is even greater when you add the heart and its circulatory system. Simply put: No blood pumping through the brain and body = no life. The heart, mind and body are certainly connected. Years ago when I consulted in private practice as a nutritionist and hypnotherapist, I worked with many people who were recovering from heart attacks, living with cancer or battling some auto-immune disease. Stating the obvious, as a nutritionist, I obviously did plenty of past and present dietary, activity and general lifestyle reviews and made recommendations. Believing in the mind-heart-body connection, I would also ask, "what event, person or situation was causing you heartache, pain, or distress within the past 24 months?" Invariably, each and every client cited something that had occurred within the prior two years that had rocked their emotional and spiritual foundation. In other words, something disrupted life as they wanted it.

So like the old riddle about the chicken and the egg, some might ask, which comes first – what is the trigger – poor diet habits, emotional distress, or from a strictly scientific level, is a disease that develops purely due to some elusive virus, bacteria or environment toxin?

Certainly there are countless external factors that can make us very ill and can possibly kill us. We need those researchers to keep on researching and seeking cures for these. Yet, for each of us as individuals, it is foolish to continue to believe that your body, mind and heart operate separately. Your body, mind and heart are one giant integrated communication platform that would humble the most advanced NASA computer engineers living today. Each makes its own music, yet they all work together in harmony.

Let's just briefly look at the miraculous nature of the human heart to hammer this point into your critical thought processes. Heart cells are being grown by stem cell researchers in labs today. Scientists don't know exactly what triggers the beating, but they acknowledge that heartbeat is self-initiated. The heart in an unborn fetus starts to beat within six weeks of conception. For the vast majority of us, the heart continues working without interruption for the next seventy to eighty years without care, cleaning, repair, or replacement. During that seventy-year lifespan it beats one hundred thousand times a day, for about forty million beats per year or nearly three billion pulsations in a lifetime. Two gallons of blood per minute, well over one hundred gallons of blood per hour are pushed through our sixty thousand mile vascular system. Which for perspective represents over two times the circumference of Planet Earth. Talk about efficiency! None of this is happenstance. All this and so much more happens in your body 24/7/365 and YOU have nothing to do with it. Or do you?

With all that perfection ordained from the minute of conception, did you ever wonder what causes a breakdown or crash? Since in modern society both refrigeration and sanitation have improved greatly, from our perspective, the majority of the illnesses we are witnessing today are the result of poor "maintenance". Inadequate nutrition and excessive caloric consumption, too much stress, not enough sleep and other bad habits -- all within our control -- are causing the high blood pressure, cardiovascular disease, heart attacks, diabetes, many cancers, auto-immune diseases and early death or disability that are affecting so many of us today.

We are now involved in a new war. The World Health Organization (WHO—and no, not the rock group!) has declared war on "non-communicable diseases" (NCD's). In case you are not familiar with the term NCD's, it is the same thing as chronic disease: heart disease, stroke, cancer, diabetes and lung conditions like asthma and emphysema. NCD's account for more than 63 percent of all deaths worldwide, killing 36 million people a year.

A recent report from the WHO said that the incidence of NCD's could be avoided or postponed. What's their maintenance plan for your vehicle? Well the basic recommendations are don't smoke, cut down your sugar intake, skip the high fat and salty processed foods, and get an annual checkup.

The top 4 can and should be incorporated by everyone immediately and the top 3 cost nothing. In fact, they would save you money! Quit smoking and cut out the refined and processed, sugar, fat and salt laden foods and its estimated that you could cut your odds of getting a NCD by greater than 80%.

Chronic diseases and obesity are not something you catch. They are conditions largely under your control and they develop from chronically poor diet and lifestyle choices. Smoking alone is estimated to be responsible for 9% of deaths worldwide. There are no numbers or estimates for deaths associated with eating a diet based around refined, processed, chemical laden manufactured foods but you can bet they are mainly responsible for the epidemic rise in NCD's and are the cause of death in more than 50% of our worldwide population.

You do not have to suffer the fate of a greatly crippled lifestyle or premature death from a preventable chronic disease. The TurboCharged perspective for becoming the master of your health destiny is three-fold:

1. *Get your mind thinking about the realities of your choices and*

their potential ramifications. Then, begin defining and making the choices that support your goals;

2. *Get your conscious and unconscious thoughts working in concert using the power of hypnosis; and,*

3. *Relieve your heart from the stress of incongruent and conflicting behaviors by ultimately uniting your body, mind and spirit.*

The TurboCharged progam is a holistic solution that will accomplish this for anyone, if the steps are followed and acted upon as outlined in the original book.

TurboCharged begins with pointing out that traditional diet advice is not working. It explains why we have all measured our results incorrectly in the past and explains how to record results in the future. Next, it moves on to teaching us the real importance of water and a fully hydrated body. The fourth step explains that there are very simple tricks that anyone can do to eliminate or forestall hunger. The program exemplifies the value of simply getting more active vs. adding more stress about the fact that you joined a gym—but have no time to get there. Moving along, *TurboCharged* details exactly which foods provide the greatest nutrition per calorie, which also happen to be the same foods that we've evolved eating throughout history. Ultimately the book concludes with the basics of visualization, self-hypnosis and affirmations that are designed to enable anyone to "see" the ultimate destination, prior to arrival. The goal of this book, *The TurboCharged Mind*, is to expand your understanding of this innate power that *TurboCharged* touched upon in Step 8, and help you to comprehend that you truly have everything you need right now to get healthier and accomplish any other goal you realistically desire and want to work towards.

The TurboCharged solution never underestimates the intimate relationship that is ongoing always between the mind, heart and body. Neither should you.

Chapter 11: *TurboCharged Mind Seeds...*

◆ A healthy body is a requirement for a healthy mind.

◆ The majority of illnesses today are called non-communicable diseases (NCDs). NCDs are chronic diseases like heart disease, stroke, cancer, diabetes and lung conditions like asthma and emphysema.

◆ The World Health Organization says NCDs can be eliminated or greatly delayed by eliminating smoking and fatty, salty, sugary junk foods.

◆ The relationship between our thoughts and emotions along with the foods that we eat daily coupled with the ways we exercise and move our bodies, plays a significant role in our health, wellbeing and our ultimate prospects for a long life.

◆ The TurboCharged program is holistic. Each step works in unison. They were designed as a result of a deep understanding of the intertwined nature of how the heart, mind and body work together perfectly with a single goal of health and wellbeing.

◆ Never underestimate the relationship and conversation that is constant between your heart, mind, and all parts of your body.

◆ The body was designed to work flawlessly for a century or greater, assuming it is cared for and maintained properly (for the instruction manual...read *TurboCharged!*)

12

Making It All Work

Hypnosis, particularly directed hypnosis, and creative visualization are very powerful tools. Make guided hypnosis a regular part of your life and you are taking the easiest route to help redirect your heart, mind and body to work together to fulfill your best possible health destiny.

To successfully attain the healthy, lean body you desire—the body that becomes the physical, visual result of your effort to reconnect your heart, mind and body working together seamlessly -- you are going to have to learn what to eat to build a strong, healthy body. You'll have to learn about other requirements for overall health as well. The best and most effective system for for this, which will also deliver rapid loss of any of your exess body fat, has been explained in our book *TurboCharged: Accelerate Your Fat Burning Metabolism, Get Lean Fast and Leave Diet and Exercise Rules in the Dust.*

If you are wondering why conscious learning is required if the subconscious and heart are so great, let me provide this little analogy: Regardless of which tools a mechanic uses, experience and knowledge remain requirements to keep any exotic car running efficiently. And, your body is the ultimate exotic vehicle.

In the preceding chapters, you learned about the benefits of hypnosis and the mind/heart/body connection. Hypnosis is the equivalent of experience. Each time you enter a state of directed hypnosis, you are unconsciously building on the conscious foundation of your experiences and knowledge. To build your best, most efficient "vehicle," you must learn better health strategies for greater strength and wellbeing, and develop an understanding of which foods will provide the most nutrition with the most efficient caloric content. These are the "tools" required for you, your body's personal "mechanic." As we point out in *TurboCharged*, which is an essential companion to this book, it is well worth your time to learn each of the eight steps in the TurboCharged™ program, as you have only one vehicle and it was created to last a lifetime. However, poor maintenance will derail performance and likely cut your "racing days" down significantly. More so, in *TurboCharged*, and it is worth repeating here, a longer, healthier life in a lean, shapely body is a first step toward a lifetime in the Winner's Circle. Crashes, like repeated bouts of ill health, diabetes, heart disease, cancer, and other debilitating diseases, begin as a result of ongoing stresses and the "poor maintenance" of the body caused by obesity, unnecessary body fat, lack of activity, lack of sleep, stress and misunderstanding of healthy food choices.

No matter how hard you try to visualize yourself as a lean, healthy, shapely person, you are going to have to make some behavior modifications to reach your goals. To make changes, you need to know what changes to make. If you've been reading carefully, you know the good news: With hypnosis, your subconscious mind will help your conscious mind process this conscious knowledge and bridge any disconnects between your desires and actions.

If you choose to work the TurboCharged steps, you will be well on your way to a leaner, healthier, stronger and more awe-inspiring physique. Every step works together to help you reach your ideal percentage of body fat and ideal body composition. The steps are all you need for success. The book you are now reading is simply Step 8 (Seeing the Prize) at full torque. *TurboCharged* and its easy to follow steps will get you up to speed and into the body of your dreams. The purpose of *The TurboCharged Mind* is to add the "punch" an engine enjoys when a car is going full speed but needs a little extra power during a race—such as when you're going 100 miles per hour but want to pass at 125!

Dieting is a word of the past. It's a well known fact that diets simply don't work. A look around proves this point. What does work, however, is TurboCharged. It has a proven 100% success rate reported by all who follow the eight simple steps.

The reasons TurboCharged works are rather simple. On most programs, when you diet, you are always waiting to stop dieting. People are constantly asking you, "How long have you been dieting? How long do you plan to continue dieting?"

TurboCharged is a holistic lifestyle. It is all about eating foods that we naturally evolved to eat, like fresh fruits and vegetables, nuts, eggs, fish, meats and some cheese, along with incorporating more activity into your daily routine. From the TurboCharged perspective, more activity can be something intentional, like choosing to take a stroll, washing your car, vacuuming your house, performing other cleaning tasks, gardening or just about anything else that gets you off your bottom, up on your legs and moving. Add a few muscle resistance workouts every couple of hours and you are well on your way to a new, sleeker and stronger physique.

In addition to the steps just discussed, TurboChargers know that fat loss is much easier with a well-hydrated body. We learn to fill our tanks often, knowing that more often than not, we are thirsty and not hungry. We work the steps to learn to recognize our thirst, differentiate it from hunger and retrain our reactions.

Hypnosis, as powerful as it is, works best in conjunction with a plan exactly like TurboCharged. By choosing to read, understand and work the TurboCharged steps, your subconscious will have a much easier time reconciling with your conscious mind the fact that eating sugary, fatty, junk foods are not in your best interest.

Remember: Your intentions—along with desires, belief and acceptance—have a major impact on whether or not you will achieve your goal. To achieve long-term success in the fat-loss and health arena, modifications are going to be necessary. The easiest route by far, with the highest success rate, is the TurboCharged route. The entire TurboCharged program is designed to make your success fast and easy. What you will learn or may have already learned by reading *TurboCharged* and *The TurboCharged Mind* sets the stage for a lifetime of greater health and wellbeing in a very lean, shapely body. For reaching any goal you desire with greater ease and speed, add a few TurboCharged meditation and hypnosis downloads to your personal program. You will be cementing your foundation for success on both the conscious and unconscious levels. This is truly a remarkable winning combination. Please keep us posted regarding your progress on our website, turbocharged.us.com and on facebook.com/turbochargedUS.

Chapter 12: TurboCharged Mind Seeds...

◈ Hypnosis is comparable to the lifetime of experience obtained by a mechanic who constantly educates him/herself.

◈ Every mechanic (including your mind) needs tools to execute work.

◈ Proper knowledge, of which foods and activities are the best substitutes for past unproductive choices, is the "tool" required to create new positive and productive habits.

◈ Everything you need to know to build a healthy, lean and strong body can be found in the highly acclaimed companion book to this one: *TurboCharged: Accelerate Your Fat Burning Metabolism, Get Lean Fast and Leave Diet and Exercise Rules in the Dust.*

◈ The TurboCharged Mind series of downloads, available at http://turbocharged.us.com/store, are the ideal guided meditations to support and direct all of your efforts for faster fat loss, a shapelier body and greater health.

◈ The remarkable power of your unconscious mind is available for your use today and every day for the rest of your life. Most people never use even 3% of their brain's immense capacity and will suffer as a consequence. You have now learned everything you need to access all your God-given power. Use it!

This book contains some pretty powerful information. Hopefully, we have been clear in explaining the amazing wealth of power contained within your subconscious mind—power that is waiting to be guided into a new and beneficial direction for improved health, greater relaxation, increased satisfaction in every aspect of your life, and greater odds of wellness and longevity.

Bibliography

The New Self-Hypnosis, by Paul Adams (1967, Parket Publishing)

Unlock Your Mind and Be Free!, by Edgar A. Barnett, MD (1979, Westwood Publishing)

Train Your Mind, Change Your Brain, by Sharon Begley (2007, Ballantine)

Induced to Produce, by Irving C. Beveridge (1995, Brentwood Christian Press)

Self-Hypnosis: Creating Your Own Destiny, by Henry Leo Bolduc (1985, Edgar Cayce Foundation)

Helping Yourself with Self-Hypnosis, Frank S. Caprio, MD & Joseph R. Berger (1963, Prentice-Hall)

The HeartMath Solution, Doc Childre and Howard Martin (1999, Harper Collins)

Creative Visualization, by Shakti Gawain (1979, Bantam)

TRANCE-formations, by John Grinder and Richard Bandler, (1981, Real People Press)

Hypnosis for Change, by Josie Hadley and Carol Staudacher (1989, New Harbinger)

The Wisdom of Milton H. Erickson, Vol. I & II, ed. by Ronald A. Havens (1992, Irvington Publishers)

The Self-Talk Solution, by Shad Helmstetter (1987, Pocket Books)

Hypnosis, by William W. Hewitt (1992, Llewellyn Publications)

Life Control, Life Enhancement, by C. Elliot Hilton, Ph.D. (1984, Radison Franklin)

Imagineering for Health, by Serge King (1981, Quest Books)

Psycho-Cybernetics, by Maxwell Maltz, MD (1969, Pocket Books)

Beyond Negative Thinking, by Joseph T. Martorano, MD and John P. Kildahl, PhD (1989, Avon Books)

Self-Hypnosis in 48 Hours, by Freda Morris (1989, Dutton)

The Theory and Practice of Hypnotism, by William J. Ousby (1966, Thorsons)

Hypnotism and the Power Within, by S. J. van Pelt (1954, Wehman Bros.)

Self Hypnosis and Other Mind-Expanding Techniques, by Charles Tebbetts (1988, Prima Publishing)

Trances People Live, by Stephen Wolinsky, Ph.D. (1991, Bramble Book)

Personal Change through Self-Hypnosis, by Pam Young (1986, The Donning Co.)

About the Authors

Dian Griesel, Ph.D., 50 chronologically, 18 metabolically, is a long-recognized health spokesperson. A dynamic and in-demand commentator since the 1980's, Dian has made guest appearances on thousands of television and radio shows. She has authored or been interviewed for articles in countless magazines, newspapers and other outlets discussing a variety of topics including: all aspects of health, wellness, stress management, diet, obesity, exercise and more. Dian is a lifetime member of the International Association of Counselors and Therapists as well as the National Guild of Hypnotists. She has served on the Board of the New York Chapter of the American Heart Association.

A serial entrepreneur, Dian has founded several businesses. A sampling include: The Business School of Happiness, a wellness and lifestyle publishing company and The Investor Relations Group (www.IRGnews.com), a nationally recognized, award-winning corporate communications firm which largely represents healthcare and high technology companies founded in 1996. Throughout the 1980s, Dian was co-partner of Spotlite Marketing, a division of Spotlite Entertainment. She marketed corporate sponsorship deals for Jay Leno, Jerry Seinfeld, Yakov Smirnoff and many other top-tier acts.

A prolific writer, in addition to co-authoring and co-developing the TurboCharged™ franchise, Dian is the author of several other books covering a plethora of topics with many more in the works. For more information, google her.

Tom Griesel, 57 chronologically, yet metabolically 17, lives his dream life as a health, wellness and rapid fat loss advisor to corporate officers, celebrities, athletes and individuals, alike. He is a Reiki Master who has also practiced Transcendental Meditation for over 30 years. Tom has been a guest on both television and radio programs hundreds of times, has consulted and lectured extensively, and has written and published and/or been interviewed thousands of times by magazines, newspapers, websites and blogs around the world.

Tom himself is the symbol of youth and a living example of health. He is a wonderful chef as well as one of the few fitness personalities who can actually demonstrate many impressive physical feats including, for example, doing 100+ push-ups in record time along with an impressive number of pull-ups as well.

In addition to co-developing the TurboCharged™ franchise, Tom co-founded The Business School of Happiness, a wellness and lifestyle publishing company. In his earlier years, he founded a health products business and he's worked in corporate America as well. In the mid-1990s, Tom was co-founder of a boutique investment banking firm that financed pharmaceutical, biotechnology and other high-tech companies that he ran successfully for twelve years.

Support for Your TurboCharged™ Lifestyle

All over the country, individuals who have read TurboCharged and applied its principles are reaping the benefits. They are living examples of its effectiveness, and people in their communities are noticing. Although the comments vary, the most frequent questions are:

"How did you get so sleek and lean?"

"What kinds of workouts are you doing to stay so toned?"

"You look amazing!"

"What can I do to look as good as you?"

"What is your secret?"

You too will find that the response you will receive from others is wonderful and feels great. There may be the occasional negative comment, but remember, any comment or suggestion that does not support your best sleek, lean, healthy body is nothing other than sour grapes from someone who doesn't have the conviction that you do. They lack the determination and drive or the knowledge that has gotten you to awe-inspiring fabulosity. Don't listen to anything that is less than positive. Simply retort, "I'm not sure if that was a compliment, but I'll take it as one. I am proud of my accomplishments." Then refer them to the book!

Since you read this book, we know you are motivated to be lean and healthy for life. Your new knowledge and awareness, along with regularly implementing the TurboCharged steps, is all you will need to keep your new body and mind free from lapsing into your old fat ways of eating and living.

Countless individuals have been able to not only lose fat but also remain at their desired body composition goal by continuing to follow all of the steps of the TurboCharged program. Others may like a little additional encouragement and community support. We have a few options for you to utilize as you wish.

TurboCharged™ Online

We want to help you keep your new lean and healthy body as a permanent and non-negotiable asset in your life. So in addition to referring to this book regularly, we invite you to join the TurboCharged online community at: www.facebook.com/TurboChargedUS. The site provides camaraderie in an online environment populated by others who, like you, have made the commitment to be sleek, lean and healthy. They no longer speak in terms of weight loss because they know that weight is merely a guideline. TurboCharged followers know that body fat is the issue. On the forum you will get ongoing inspiration and ideas from us and be able to chat with others. You will be kept up-to-date on any new significant research that further validates and might ultimately be incorporated into the TurboCharged program.

On TurboCharged.us.com, you will also find all sorts of videos showing you new fun ways to incorporate activity into your life. You will also find delicious TurboCharged recipes, new mini-minute exercise ideas, chat, support and encouragement.

We hope you join us and invite your friends too. Please log in and visit often. We want to know you and cheer your success.

Dian and Tom log in regularly to provide insight and encouragement. The site provides a great forum to exchange ideas, discuss new trends, exchange recipes, ask questions about specific challenges or problems, and confirm which foods will contribute to your progress or not. For those of you who are into Cruise Control, there's plenty of daily talk and ideas on how to easily keep your fat loss permanent.

You can also follow us at www.twitter.com/diangriesel. We aggregate broad range compilation of articles and videos regarding health, stress management, happiness and general well-being.

A Prototype Plan for Creating Your Own TurboCharged™ Community

Some people prefer human contact and commiseration for support. For you, we think that a support group just might be the answer. We want to provide you with some ideas that others have used to find like-minded TurboCharged advocates and a plan for making it effective.

A support group can provide its members with an opportunity for mutual growth and exchange. Members can share similar difficulties and feelings, and offer each other personal perspectives for resolving those difficulties or working through those feelings. Groups allow members the experience of learning that others face similar challenges. The exchange of knowledge and ideas promotes progress. Members can share their goals with the optimistic goals of others in the group so they can cheer each other's progress as they move forward as a community. A support group also provides encouragement when members encounter, such as the occasional plateaus, and offers different strategies for success in meeting goals.

Support groups can be structured or informal. Group members can meet and decide on the preferred style. Often a group begins simply as a walking club with two members. Before long, others want to join the fun as they watch the fat dropping.

Some groups meet daily for walks and then weekly for conversation and comparing progress. Others establish a monthly meeting at a set location and often plan it at a restaurant that serves TurboCharged foods and they make it a communal dining experience.

Group leaders can establish a planned agenda, or the format can be kept casual. Regardless of the style, groups can provide tremendous support and therefore add to the likelihood of ongoing success for all those involved.

The most successful groups follow certain basic rules:

◈ The environment needs to be warm and nonjudgmental so attendees are free to speak without embarrassment.

◈ The T.H.I.N.K. Rule should apply to any comments:

T: Is the comment Thoughtful

H: Is the comment Hurtful

I: Is the comment Intelligent and in line with Turbo-Charged thinking

N: Is the comment Necessary

K: Is the comment Kind and encouraging of the success of others.

◈ Confidentiality must be respected. Personal disclosures must be kept confidential within the group.

◈ Medical opinions should be avoided. Medical advice is best dispensed by an individual's personal doctor after a good blood work-up.

◈ Personal experiences can be shared.

◈ Group leaders should rotate. By sharing the leadership task, everyone gets a sense of belonging and participation. Group leaders have a role of keeping the conversation moving, interesting and lively. No one individual should be allowed to dominate the discussion.

◈ Respect differences. It is important that group leaders encourage participation by all leaders—but don't force sharing. Some people learn by listening. Others will be more compelled to share regularly and often.

To get your group going, the steps are simple:

1. For starters, establish a leader if necessary; decide how that leadership will rotate.

2. Decide how large you want the group to be. As others see your success and you tell them to "read the book" your circle will likely grow. Look for members through like-minded friends, work, church, social groups and exercise facilities.

3. Choose how often you will meet: Daily for walks, weekly or monthly for chat.

4. Select a meeting place: A participant's home, church, restaurant, school, town hall or library.

5. Get everyone's contact information: name, telephone number, email address, mailing address.

6. Define your confidentiality and respect for other policies.

7. Determine the meeting format: Will food be allowed? Will each member be responsible for some aspect of a TurboCharged meal? Will the meeting be formal with an agenda or a casual gathering to chat? Will a specific topic be the focus of each meeting? Etc.

The most important aspects of any support group are the encouragement, support, community and progress reports of participants. Don't worry if your first meeting seems a little stilted. Lively discussion and exchange will increase as trust does within the community.

It is important to remember that you want to gain insight into your own behaviors, and receive and give feedback, support, knowledge and encouragement to each other. You aren't there to get "fixed" or "fix" others. We all come with our own perspectives (food-related and otherwise) and reach our own realities whenever we are ready.

One way of beginning is to have the group leader start with a discussion of "their story": a bit of past history struggling with weight and the end of that search once they began the Turbo-Charged program. No one should be forced to speak, but gently encouraged to share, if they are comfortable.

Conversations can get very lively if you ask participants to report the numbers from their body fat scales: Weight, Body Fat %, Water and Metabolic Age. As group members notice others not just getting leaner but also younger, enthusiasm levels can really rise.

Members should be encouraged to share any material they determine to be relevant to the group: Maybe an article in a newspaper or magazine. Another failed fat celebrity who dieted yet gained it all back (yes—this is both fun gossip and motivating. You'll realize fame doesn't bring leanness!). Recipes that really fit the TurboCharged program. Products to enhance a TurboCharged lifestyle. Coupons regarding sales of TurboCharged supporting items. Community calendars and maybe information about a walk to raise money for a community event, etc.

"Buddies" are a common practice in certain support groups. Sometimes a buddy is selected for a period of time to help initiate a new member into the group. Buddies can be great. Sometimes buddies are a pain in the butt! Basically the concept of buddy is that you will each share your personal story more intimately. Having buddies is yet another decision for the group to decide to implement or not.

Support groups can provide great motivational enhancement to the TurboCharged program. We know people who have started them at their yoga center, office, church group and within countless other formats. Some members will be more competitive within the group than others and you can use them to everyone's inspirational advantage as you all watch them exceed their previously stated goals.

To be TurboCharged is a new way of life. It is the perfect holistic program that positions you for success not just today but for the rest of your life. With your support group in place, you and your group can all get and feel better, sleeker, leaner, healthier and more fabulous together!

TurboCharged™ Learning Programs

TurboCharged™, developed by Dian Griesel, Ph.D. and Tom Griesel, provides simple, proven strategies—with no supplements, gimmicks or special equipment—that cause rapid loss of excess body fat while improving overall health. It is an eight step program that incorporates highly nutritious and natural foods and utilizes a wonderful understanding of human nature and natural, common sense to accomplish greater health, leaner bodies and a distinct sense of better well-being.

Explore and experience the depth of the TurboCharged program with additional books, music, downloads, hypnosis downloads and advanced learning programs.

The TurboCharged program and products can be used by individuals, small groups, or organizations to learn and sustain the necessary skills to maintain a lean healthy body and better physical and mental health.

For a free catalog of our complete TurboCharged product line or information on volume discounts, call 860-619-0177 or write to:

TurboCharged
c/o The Business School of Happiness
PO Box 302
Washington Depot, CT 06794

You can also visit our website: www.turbocharged.us.com to see our current product offerings.

TurboCharged™ Books
Authored by America's New First Family of Health,
siblings Dian Griesel, Ph.D. & Tom Griesel

The entire TurboCharged™ Series is designed to work with your busy, hectic, time-crunched lifestyle.

Books include:

TurboCharged: Accelerate Your Fat Buring Metabolism, Get Lean Fast and Leave Diet and Exercise Rules in the Dust

Learn how eight easy steps make it possible for you to permanently lose excess body fat faster than you can possibly imagine while simultaneously improving your health.

You'll be learning why conventional diet and exercise advice is causing our obesity epidemic, eating healthy and delicious foods that provide the perfect fuel for energy while keeping your body in fat-burning mode, skipping aerobic exercise, reducing stress, cravings and anxiety and increasing relaxation.

Not a diet but a lifestyle, TurboCharged is the ultimate program for accommodating busy schedules while providing the secret roadmap for living life lean and healthy.

"TurboCharged doesn't bog down the reader with lots of science. Instead, it tells you what to do, when to do it, and if you follow the very simple guidelines, you too will be dropping fat fast, leaning out and attaining your goal of a lower body-fat percentage, decreases in inches and a younger metabolic age. TurboCharged is a system designed with genetics in mind and based on sound science. With a combination like that, you can't fail."

-Fred Pescatore, MD, MPH, CCN
Author of *The Hamptons Diet*

TurboCharged Recipes: Delicious Fuel for Your Fabulous Fat Burning Machine

This book is filled with hundreds of recipes for those TurboChargers who want to stay in Cruise Control for life. The simple-to-follow recipes make maintaining a lean, healthy, fabulous physique easier than ever. For those who desire to feed themselves, their families and friends well, from simple dinners to entertaining crowds, this book provides the quick go-to answers for delicious snacks, appetizers, drinks, dinners, desserts and more. Novice to professional chefs will enjoy creating a variety of meals designed to help all dieters to stay on the TurboCharged road to Leandom.

365 TurboCharged Days

This book contains 365 days of motivation. Each day offers a new explanation in a fun and interesting way that supports the scientific basis behind the TurboCharged™ solution for permanent fat-loss and a leaner, healthier body for life.

Designed in a way that the reader can begin this book at any time of the year, for TurboChargers, wanna-be TurboChargers, and the yet-to-be converted – 365 TurboCharged Days is the ultimate companion to educate, inspire, and support the goal of a lean, awe-inspiring physique in the Winner's Circle of Health.

The TurboCharged™ Hypnosis Download Series
Written and Recorded by Dian Griesel, PhD.

We all talk to ourselves. Yet, much of this conversation is negative.

Hypnosis is a powerful technique that you can use to achieve positive changes in thinking and behavior…fast! All hypnosis is self-hypnosis. It can be easily learned and practiced by anyone. It is magical in many ways because it enables your brain to slow down and enter the alpha range, which is where dreams occur. As you enter this realm of relaxed, altered consciousness—the daydreaming state—you can make your self-directed dreams become realities.

Like daydreaming, hypnosis is a perfectly normal, safe and healthy phenomenon. The only real difference between hypnosis and fantasizing or daydreaming is that in a state of hypnosis, you mind is specifically directed and focused on the beneficial goals you wish to achieve. Hypnosis is beneficial for anyone who could use some additional rest and relaxation. The worst that can happen from listening to any hypnosis download is that you will be more relaxed and productive! That isn't so bad, is it?

TurboCharged Beginner Meditation

This free beginner directed meditation is designed to help introduce listeners to the power of self-hypnosis, guided meditation and subsequent relaxation. It can aid greatly in assisting you to achieve a happier, more peaceful and more productive life.

TurboCharged Fat Loss

Accelerate your excess fat loss and shape up your body with this innovative hypnosis download that will work for your body because it works with your mind. While experiencing deep relaxation, you will eliminate your destructive eating habits using techniques that have been specifically created for rapid fat loss and ultimate health. This download is the ultimate companion to the book, TurboCharged: Accelerate Your Fat Burning Metabolism, Get Lean Fast and Leave Diet and Exercise Rules in the Dust.

Depressurized the TurboCharged Way

Within minutes you will begin to sense relaxation throughout your entire body. Shortly thereafter worries and concerns will be stored away, as if placed in a box high up on a shelf, only to be retrieved if absolutely necessary. Experience the power and willingness of your mind and body to connect and relax, to feel great and let go, as you learn powerful new techniques to deal with any stressful situation with a coat of protective armor.

TurboCharged Energy

Anger, fear, guilt, worry and anxiety imprison the mind. These are very normal emotions, yet, left unchecked they can cripple lives and health. Imagine having new mind expanding techniques and new ways to see everything from a more loving and positive perspective. This download is Dian's personal favorite. She has personally used it daily for many years.

TurboCharged Sleep

With this hypnosis download, each night you can leave your cares behind and get the sleep you really need. You will be guided to a state of deeply relaxed selective awareness and be taught how to relax for a more restful sleep. You will easily learn personal techniques to release the worries and tension that can build up during the day. This download gives your mind, body and emotions positive direction and results in deeper, better and more refreshing sleep.

TurboCharged to Quit Smoking Now

Contrary to what you may believe, smoking does not help you relax; it increases tension. It doesn't help you think more clearly; it actually causes brain lapses and nervousness as the nicotine circulates in your bloodstream. Smoking causes cancer and heart disease, and it is hurtful to your children.

You can be a nonsmoker. Twenty minutes after quitting, your heart rate and blood pressure will improve. Within twelve hours, carbon monoxide levels in your blood return to normal. Within a year, the excess risk of coronary heart disease will be half that of a smokers.

With this hypnosis download, becoming a nonsmoker is easy and effortless. Some people will quit after their first session. Most will continue listening for years for the easy reinforcement and relaxation pleasure this session provides. Choose to become a nonsmoker today!

Be sure to log in at www.TurboCharged.US.com to see all of our new hypnosis downloads that are coming soon...

TurboCharged™ Retreats, Seminars & Training Programs

TurboCharged™ training programs are specifically designed to provide tools and techniques that increase the understanding of how the body works, the requirements of health and how to keep a body lean in the most nutritious, energizing, and effective ways. The tools and techniques—designed for practical use in situations characterized by information overload, time pressure and stress—result in greater long-term success, reduce frustration, fight diet burnout, and ameliorate physical symptoms of stress and negative moods so often associated with traditional dieting.

TurboCharged via its publisher/parent company, The Business School of Happiness Inc., provides lectures, retreats, seminars and both on and off-site programs to help individuals and organizations discover and sustain the use of the TurboCharged solution. The flagship organizational program, has a modular design that can be customized to fit an organization's specific business and time objectives.

For more information on trainings and seminars, call 860-619-0177 or write to:

TurboCharged
c/o The Business School of Happiness
PO Box 302
Washington Depot, CT 06794

TurboCharged™ Refrigerator Magnet

Go to the store at www.turbocharged.us.com and order your TurboCharged magnet to stick on your refrigerator or wherever it is most helpful.

It says…

STOP!

Are You Really Hungry
or
Just Thirsty?

Have a Big Drink of Water.

Make it a *TurboCharged*™ Day!

Write to the Authors

Although we cannot guarantee that every letter written to Dian Griesel, Ph.D. and Tom Griesel will be individually answered, all will be forwarded. They appreciate hearing from readers and learning about your enjoyments, thoughts and benefits from the TurboCharged program.

You can contact Dian and Tom at www.turbocharged.us.com or by sending a letter to:

Dian Griesel, Ph.D. or Tom Griesel
c/o The Business School of Happiness Inc.
PO Box 302
Washington Depot, CT 06794

Request Important Free
TurboCharged™ Updates

Let TurboCharged send you, your relatives and friends the latest TurboCharged News Bulletins on health and nutrition discoveries. Periodically, you'll get recipes, cutting edge science information about health, rapid fat loss, exercise, stress management and longevity, new ways to accelerate your metabolism and more.

Send us your email address or your full address. Please neatly print each address.

Mail to:
TurboCharged
c/o Business School of Happiness
PO Box 302
Washington Depot, CT 06794

Or, Log onto www.turbocharged.us.com and sign up yourself and others.

- -

Name_____

Address_____

City_____State_____ Zip Code_____

Email_____

www.ingramcontent.com/pod-product-compliance
Lightning Source LLC
Chambersburg PA
CBHW072235290326
41934CB00008BA/1306